DOMINATE YOUR DAY

DOMINATE YOUR DAY

A High Performer's Guide to Winning at Life

CHRIS WARNES

Warrior Consulting
Milford, Connecticut

Dominate Your Day
A High Performers Guide to Winning at Life

Chris Warnes.

Copyright © 2021 Christopher Warnes

Photography © 2021 Paola Santamaria

Design cover by Paola Santamaria

ISBN-13: 978-0-578-30010-8
First printing October 2021

DEDICATION

To my mother, Nanci, who has not only single-handedly taught me my tireless work ethic but has sacrificed her comforts, well-being, and at times, her health to provide me with an opportunity to create what I have.

Mom, you're the most beautiful, passionate, caring, selfless, loving, protective, fittest mom—my number one since day one. "Thank you" is an understatement. I only hope I can return what you've given me in life.

CONTENTS

CONTENTS

INTRODUCTION

This is only the third time I've publicly written about this life-changing day. It took me 13 years to muster up the courage to share this.

Fourteen years ago was the closest I came to death.

Fourteen years ago, my platoon was on patrol to locate two soldiers who had gone missing and who were later found to have been kidnapped by our opposing forces.

Kidnapped. That doesn't happen in war these days. It makes national and world news when it happens, as this situation did.

Watching yourself on *CNN World News* is a sight and a memory I'll never forget.

It was a hot day, around 130 degrees. We were all on edge and wanted blood. We knew who took them, and we were driving right up to their base in the hope of a fight.

And a fight is what we found.

I was at the front of the convoy of five gun trucks as the lead gunner for my platoon in a heavily armored truck built to withstand explosions. I was in the gun turret and was the only man who could see, hear and smell outside of our truck.

The day was long, hot and dreadful. We moved slowly, looking for our brothers.

And then I caught the distinct smell of death. Anyone who's smelled human death knows exactly what it is. There's no mistaking it.

I dropped back down into the truck and said, "Stop, I smell death," and we stopped. My boss, Sergeant Jones, hopped on the radio…and told his boss.

Then his boss called his boss…and so on.

The orders we received were to carry on and press forward as a convoy, starting with our truck at the front.

As we pressed forward, I'd never felt so much pain.

In that instant, our truck was hit by an IED, which was my 11th direct hit on that tour.

But this one was different.

It was a monster. The hole in the road was so big, no one could drive the road. Our truck landed about 70 feet away, off the road, tumbling through the air before landing.

I have vivid memories of looking out of the gun turret, seeing the sky and then the ground several times as we barrel rolled through the air.

The pain was mind-blowing. I reached down to see if my "package" was still attached and started smiling as it was. Anyone who's been blown up can relate to what starts as an uncertain moment that turns into complete happiness.

Our truck was blown in half, but I could still climb out of the gun turret. I was confused, in shock, disoriented, bleeding out of my face and back, in pain, but knew I needed to exit the vehicle.

Before I did, I had two goals in mind: first to check on everyone in the truck to see if they were alive and then to find my machine gun, a 25-pound Squad automatic weapon also known as the "SAW," which I'd named Piglet, as she was very much a pig. I climbed out of the turret, as did the others, to be met by the rest of the platoon who couldn't believe we were actually alive.

We were treated and then evacuated from the fight. The next day, our sister platoon went down the same road, starting from the other end of the route, finding our brothers lying on the side of the road about 20 feet from the massive IED that nearly killed us. They were decapitated, dismembered, castrated and burned.

On top of the mutilation, their bodies lay on top of two more monstrous IEDs designed as booby traps to maim or kill whoever found them.

After a quick recovery, I was awarded a Purple Heart. I wear my Purple Heart proudly and since then was nicknamed "Hard to Kill," as many have tried, and yet I'm still here.

This is the reality of the world we live in—not the majority of humans, but there are some. Make no mistake. There is and always has been evil living with us.

That day, June 18, 2006, my perspective changed forever and I now live a grateful man, thankful to wake up and live a life full of purpose, knowing I do so because the scariest day of my life taught me all I need to know.

To hear the whole story, go to *chriswarnes.com*. Click the podcast tab and select Episode One.

I spent the first 20 years of life unsure which direction to travel, what decisions to make, where to go or what to do. In hindsight, I didn't know I could be a leader until I entered the military. Prior, I was more concerned with winning the attention of those around me and hoping they'd like me.

My early decision-making was led by wanting my actions to be appreciated by others, in this case, friends. I now know this was simply the wrong way of going about my day to day, but it took finding the leader within to realize this.

In 2008 when leaving the military, I was still unclear what I wanted in life. I loved what I did in the Army and would never trade my service for anything this world offers. However, I knew I was done. I was meant for bigger things in life. I knew I couldn't work for anyone long-term again. I could no longer be led unless there was a serious leader whom I respected.

Leaders of this magnitude are not only few and far between, but are something of the past as I observe the world today. Leadership at this level is challenging. With many other qualities, hard work scares off most as they're comfortable complaining about the average lives they live, sitting back being a victim of their circumstances rather than actively taking control.

Now, as a civilian, life was very different; society and the economy had changed. There was an overall sense of entitlement and mass victim-playing after the Great Recession. I had no clue what to make of it or how to deal with it all, other than focusing on developing myself.

It was clear I saw the world differently than most and I began to use this unique vision to my advantage.

I became a personal trainer after separating from the military, and that's where it all began, over a decade of mistake after mistake, lesson after lesson, heartbreak after heartbreak, and what seemed to be, at the time of the never-ending painful process of trying to get by, making a living for myself, self-employed, surviving rather than growing. During the first six to eight years, I had a mindset that held me back from achieving wealth and success and a perspective that wouldn't allow me to progress. My ego was my arch-rival, and I didn't know it.

Life, your job and business can be fun, full of prosperity and abundance. Over 14 years as an entrepreneur, I've built five companies that were successful and prosperous, employing hundreds along the way and creating eight figures of revenue.

I had the pleasure of teaching countless students to build and scale their own companies too. I hope you'll learn how to build your life or business, experiencing more fun, prosperity, abundance and success in your work and life.

In this book, you'll learn from the seven biggest mistakes and lessons from my climb in life, mostly as an entrepreneur who created a life of spirituality, time and financial freedom, abundance, prosperity and strong relationships. I want this for you too, and this is why I wrote this book, for you to learn from the path I took that led to an open door I walked through.

I hope you walk through your door too.

As you learn from the chapters and step away from this book, you'll have many new experiences as a human. You'll learn more about yourself than most care to know, and learn to have more fun in life as you recognize what you truly want. You'll have more fun; you'll make more money, have stronger relationships, ease in your day to day and success, developing your mindset along the way.

I hope these lessons I learned show how I've overcome and eliminated bad habits and that you can also do this, eliminating old behaviors and habits keeping you from all the good you can bring into your life.

It took realizing that mistakes are great before I could learn each lesson. Once we embrace the idea that mistakes will free us from ourselves, not only is freedom near, but so is a beautiful jewel of life: peace of mind. A wise man once told me that a mistake is only a lesson; learn the lesson, and that's where the growth lies.

A book can stimulate our thoughts, which is the greatest service any book can give. The purpose of this particular book is to stimulate your thoughts—thoughts free from bias and prejudice, seeking truth no matter where or how it may be found.

CHAPTER 1

EVERYTHING IS YOUR FAULT
ACCEPTING RESPONSIBILITY FOR YOUR ACTIONS

There will always be the 99-to-1 rule, the one example that doesn't apply to most of what we're talking about. There will be situations and circumstances you have no control over and aren't your fault. It isn't your fault you were raped, molested as a child, were hit from behind in a car accident, stopped at a red light or found yourself in the middle of the Boston Marathon bombing. These are examples of the one percent.

We'll focus on the 99 percent that most of the things you do in your life and mess up are your fault. It's your fault you were late; it wasn't traffic. It was your fault you got the order wrong, you didn't take the time to order well enough or ensure you communicated what you wanted sufficiently to get the correct order.

It's your fault if you're in a job you hate—you accepted it. It's your fault you're in a toxic relationship and you're miserable. There isn't anyone holding a gun to your head to stay in a bad situation. If you're unhappy, it's your fault, not your girlfriend, not your boyfriend, not your husband…not your wife's fault. It's not your boss' fault, not your manager, not your coworkers; it's your fault. It's all your fault.

The truth is a hard pillow to swallow, especially when written or spoken in black and white. However, cold showers of truth always have the growth and answers you're looking for on the other side when you accept it. Go to *chriswarnes.com* and click the podcasts tab, Episode 50, "You're the Problem."

Once we realize the growth we desire is on the other side of tough conversations and after accepting responsibilities for our actions, we'll QUICKLY notice how much smoother life becomes. Let's use an example. You're driving down the road at 45 mph in a 35mph zone. A police officer clocked you on a radar gun, and then pulled in behind you and…you guessed it, pulled you over.

Like you, I'd be upset—now I'm late and worse, may get a ticket for speeding. First, if you're pleasant and respectful, your day will be much better. Every police officer I know has told me this. The moment you don't follow directions, you lack respect, raise your voice or worse, don't follow orders, your day will likely get much worse. So, now you're dealing with being late and a potential ticket, if not a few depending on how you act.

Many of us—including me years ago—would become upset and point the finger at the officer for the ticket, after delivering the cold hard truth, "You were traveling at 45 mph, 10 mph over the speed limit in a posted 35 mph zone. Your brake light is out, and your tints are illegal. Here's a ticket, have a nice day."

Now, this is where the successful separate themselves from the non-successful. A successful person will learn where the mistakes were made. Okay, I was speeding, which is my fault. When I got the tints, I knew they were illegal—also my fault—and I should have inspected my car better to know my brake light was out. This was a valuable and costly lesson and I'm going to learn from it and thank the officer for keeping me, and more importantly, the community safe.

Successful people first accept responsibility for their actions, which is the most challenging part. Then they look for the opportunity within the mistake to learn from. Lastly, they unpack the error, learn the lesson, add it to the memory banks and move on. Unsuccessful people do, well, the opposite.

When we fail to take responsibility for our actions, we find it easiest to point the finger at everyone else. Of course, it's the officer's fault. Why would it be mine? That's the too-easy option of pointing the finger. But in most cases, the same finger pointing to the officer is the finger that can be taught to be pointed inward where it belongs.

I want to give you an example of a situation I didn't take responsibility for until nearly 13 years after it happened. It may have been the most traumatic event that ever happened to me and it completely changed my perspective on life. As you read in the introduction, I was wounded in combat on my first of two tours in Iraq. That was the most brutal day of my life, considering I was 20 years old, and thought I was going to die.

The real gold in this story is that I use this lesson to teach you that getting wounded was my fault. Yes, you read that correctly: my fault, not the fault of those who were trying to kill me that day. When you think about a trauma, you might actually see things differently and believe it may have been your fault. Now, let me explain.

Let's look at the situation objectively for a moment. The people who attacked us that day, along with every other Islamic extremist I faced during my two tours, thought what they were doing was the right thing to do.

Because of their extreme religious beliefs, they felt they were doing as Allah was directing them through the interpretations of their beliefs. Their beliefs stemmed from other extremists teaching these practices or from their circle of influence, family, church, friends and recruitment propaganda. They thought what they were doing while here on this earth was what they were supposed to be doing, which was hunting and killing American Christians on their holy ground. Sad, however, is the logical explanation of their actions in layman's terms.

Now let's discuss how the event was my fault and how freeing it was to learn and accept this: I SIGNED UP FOR THE ARMY, and even more, for the Infantry.

For those not familiar with the Infantry, this is the Wikipedia definition: "Infantry is a military specialization that engages in military combat on foot, distinguished from cavalry, artillery, and armored forces.

Also known as foot soldiers or infantrymen, Infantry traditionally relies on moving by foot between combats and may also use mounts, military vehicles, or other transport. The job of an infantryman is described as "Members of the Infantry are ground troops that engage with the enemy in close-range combat. They operate weapons and equipment to engage and destroy enemy ground forces. This job is typically considered the job in the military that's more physically demanding and psychologically stressful than any other job."

What were the chances I would face an enemy combatant with my job selection? Very high, and thus I did, often. It was my choice to sign up for the Army when the most powerful country is at war with not one but two other countries, Iraq and Afghanistan. It was my choice to pick a combat job. It was my choice to serve the country. It was my choice to fight rather than run. It was my responsibility I was wounded, one of the toughest yet most freeing pills I've ever swallowed.

This will release you too, as soon as you decide you're open to it.

"A hero is someone who understands the responsibility
that comes with his freedom."
~ **Bob Dylan**

HOW TO POINT THE FINGER INWARD

When we understand that the person who looks back at us in the mirror is the root of our problems, we understand that the most challenging answers that haunt us are of our own creation. Our minds can be a prison with bars locking us into self-inflicted torture or a beautiful, well-manicured grassy field, with flowing flowers along with gold bars, piles of money, health and all we desire. The difference is that we feed our minds along with the thoughts that go through it.

Make no mistake, it's your choice if you're happy or sad, poor or wealthy, abundant or famished. Within your mind, you control what you see in the mirror. One of the hardest things to accept is that what you see is a unique, powerful, beautiful or handsome human with endless opportunities in front of you. The first step is believing this. The second step is pointing the finger inward or in the case of looking in the mirror, pointing the finger at what you see.

Pointing your finger inward is incredibly freeing. You'll free yourself from blaming others for your problems and open yourself up to truths. Truths are what we might not want to hear. However, they're just that: the truth. Initially, they hurt a lot. After a while, they free you further.

There's a story I always tell about having had truth delivered to me—the cold, hard, tough-to-swallow truth, long after I took responsibility for my actions and pointed the finger inward, freeing myself. At least, I thought I was free before this conversation when I questioned myself and if I actually had gotten past my ego.

About 11 years into my entrepreneurial journey, I decided it was time to hire a mentor. I needed direction and to hold myself accountable. Months later, I was having a conversation with a mentor and in that conversation, he told me I was selfish. I didn't think it was true, and it shook me to the core. I hadn't heard that word and my name together in the same sentence since I was a teenager. I didn't believe it. I argued, and my ego came out in full force to protect my feelings.

We were talking about leadership. He was asking how I lead my companies and my staff. He said I wasn't focused on developing my team personally in their lives. I was focused on job performance, growing our company primarily and helping them personally secondarily. I couldn't wrap my head around this and fought it until I gave in, stepped past my ego and understood that developing my staff to grow the company ultimately was a selfish act.

There are dozens of excuses I could give as to why I did this, including that their mortgages have to be paid, along with providing food for their families. However, I accepted the truth, pointed the finger inward and freed myself from these selfish acts. I learned in that one conversation how I was leading could use improvement.

From that moment, my team's personal development was the number one priority. I found that basic skills such as discipline, health, scheduling, exercise, goal setting, mindset work, budgeting and even communication were topics I had worked with students on, but assumed my team understood too. Then I faced myself in the mirror and pointed the finger inward to understand I could do better at not assuming and, in turn, could teach my team better.

THE ONE-PERCENT EXAMPLE

March 16th, 2020, 11:00 a.m. It's fair to say I saw this coming. I watched my business customer numbers fall almost 90%. Before then, we'd have about 500 people a day through our doors on a busy day until the week prior, when that number fell to about 50 on a busy day.

The media beautifully executed scare tactics surrounding the COVID 19 coronavirus, which was the scariest thing to hit this world since the meteor that hit the earth millions of years ago, wiping out all living life, including the dinosaurs.

That morning, one of my staff, who stood by me, helped build our fantastic company and followed my lead for almost three years, said the dreaded words I'll always remember, "Chris, did you see Facebook?" In my per usual dry, joking and sarcastic manner, I responded, "No, what did Zuck do to kill his stock this time?"

Even being a sarcastic guy, I knew in my gut what her answer would be, no matter if I was ready to hear it or not. "The governor said we have to close our doors by 8:00 pm tonight." I checked Facebook and read a statement from our Governor Ned Lamont articulating this message that all nonessential businesses must close to "flatten the curve" and spread of COVID for 14 days.

I knew right then many things would change, including capitalism as we knew it and the fitness industry I was in. But I thought I could outwork the circumstances of having to close a brick-and-mortar company I'd put my entire 20s and half my 30s into building, owning and operating.

However, I couldn't outwork the circumstances created around me, no matter how much work I put in. The events I had to adapt to, so did the entire world, a "global pandemic" that crippled the whole global economy. There was well-planned media propaganda to drive fear to the ordinary-minded people of the world, covering up the fact, not only did the United States of America and our economy have to correct, quickly hitting a depression, but so did the rest of the world.

This is a perfect example of the 1% rule on display: One percent of things in our life that happen to us are outside our control and responsibility. Ninety-nine percent of situations that occur are our responsibility. The long-term effects are directly related to how we deal with those situations with our choices.

DENIAL OF THE ONE-PERCENT RULE

Over the next 90 days, I worked a white patch into my beard, noticing first on the left side of my face within 30 days and then on the right side of my face by 60 days. As a 34-year-old man, I enjoy wearing a beard with my salt-and-pepper look, but now I was looking more like Santa Claus than myself.

Looking back on the situation, my ego was telling me I could push through this "pandemic," hold off shutdown and everything would be okay. As an eternal optimist, I always look for the bright side of things or a lens of focus to frame situations to see the positive.

As a self-aware human, no matter how internally aware we are, our ego is still powerful and can and will be controlling. Even seasoned businesspeople, seasoned people in life, self-aware people can be tricked into thinking the one-percent rule doesn't apply to us.

As time went by, past the 90 days the state shut down the business and our state economy, we were given the green light to reopen into phase two. Thirty days after reopening, I realized the situation was not in my hands any longer as the customer was frankly too scared to come into a gym, given the scare tactics of mainstream and social media platforms scaring everyone about COVID.

Looking at live data, as I did, can save you a lot of time, heartache and money because numbers never lie; people do. By day 60 of reopening, I knew I had to close my dream. What took me eight years of working toward using all of my time, money and effort was over and I reached out to my mentor, Thomas Plummer, to ask for clarity. The answer was simple—if you want to hear my interview with him, YouTube, "Chris Warnes Episode 74—The Why, with Special Guest Thomas Plummer."

Thomas reinforced the knowledge that this decision had nothing to do with what I'd done, and everything to do with the environment the fitness industry is in, as well as the state of our economy and my local market given the COVID situation.

The one-percent rule does apply, but it only applies for situations entirely out of your control. At times, it will take someone in your life who knows you well to break it to you that the one-percent rule applies to what you're dealing with, especially if you're a high performer used to taking responsibilities for your actions or the actions of those around you.

CHAPTER 2

BEING WRONG WILL FREE YOU

It's natural for average humans to think they're never wrong. With no data to back up this statement—it's only from observation throughout life—I've found a pattern among most people who will do anything to pass the blame, point the finger and even lie to avoid being wrong and looking "bad" in front of others.

I'd also venture to say the majority of people I've watched throughout life, state to state, country to country, at times don't even know they're trying to escape blame for something simple, but freedom is on the other side of accepting the fault. Admitting wrongdoing was incredibly hard for me from the start, mainly due to my environment growing up. Environment shapes our ideas, beliefs, and while young, our choices. As a child, if I was wrong, I was punished. As a young adult, I thought a punishment came with mistakes.

However, we get what we focus on and I focused on getting better around my mid- to late-20s. The environment you were raised in, with few exceptions, shaped your thoughts, beliefs, perceptions, opinions and views. When the day comes when you're ready to face yourself, your shortcomings, along with understanding the road to healing may be long, it will also free you from the most important person, yourself.

As time went on, I realized people depended on me to teach them simple things in life and also some hard things, like being wrong. As I grew as a man—let alone a businessman—I found I loved building teams; these teams were my staff. I took an interest in developing them personally and professionally. However, once the staff grew to upward of 60, I needed to teach on a grander scale, not only one on one, but in group classes.

Once realized, I'd hold meetings and put myself on display to teach whatever the lesson might be, including being wrong. I love teaching this lesson. I'm wrong daily and would use the silliest "I was wrong example" to bring everyone together and teach them how I was wrong.

THE FIRST STEP OF BEING WRONG: ACCEPTING RESPONSIBILITY

The first thing you must learn is to be okay with being wrong. It's okay; it really is. It's freeing to be incorrect. It can be challenging for many. However, the more you open up to it, the more you'll allow yourself to be wrong, and the more you allow yourself to be wrong, the more you'll learn. Being wrong is educational; you're learning how not to do something wrong again if you're open to it.

A wise man once told me that being wrong is nothing more than learning a lesson—and how valid those words were. When we want to learn, we create endless opportunities for ourselves. When we create endless possibilities for ourselves, we set ourselves up for success. It's the only choice moving forward that will be the determining factor if opportunities become successful.

The choice to be wrong will free you from yourself and the mundane, average mindset and thinking. If you're still struggling to understand the concept that being wrong is okay and accepting responsibility for a mistake, go back and reread Chapter One, re-implementing accepting responsibility for your actions. It may help to go to *chriswarnes.com* and select the podcast tab, Episode 50: "You're the Problem."

SECOND STEP TO BEING WRONG: WHERE WAS THE MISTAKE?

The key to the mistake, after we accept it, is to identify where we went wrong. This is sometimes the most challenging part because our ego shields our logical thinking mind, making excuses to justify our action and outright blocks us from seeing the mistake. Most people are unaware of how egocentric they are. It's dangerous how clueless the majority is, blocking us from many things, to include how wrong we are.

We free ourselves when we adopt the mindset that we can be wrong and that we're actually often wrong, especially at the beginning of the transition into that way of thinking. Our minds open up to lessons and knowledge that comes along with it. This is called "shifting the lens of focus."

The previous lens of focus was, "I'm never wrong, nor can I be," and the lens of focus shifted to, "I can be and am often wrong." You'll begin to look for opportunities where you are or were wrong. Thinking about some of the most difficult decisions you've made or been a part of is an excellent place to start.

I like to use the example of a man who believes he's happily married. Then, suddenly a bomb drops in his lap one day that his wife isn't happy and wants to or is filing for a divorce. Was the man wrong? Yes, he was, and this is why. Even though it came as a surprise to him, he's mistaken for taking his situation for granted, not appreciating her. In the traditional sense, he never listened to her. Women are an emotionally based gender who love to express how they feel. When men decide to not listen because a football game is on or they're busy working or out with their friends, they're dismissing her and saying, "I don't care."

Women will only take so much of this before they've had it. They want a man who's centered and will hear them no matter the situation. The self-centered man isn't listening to his partner and shouldn't be surprised when she leaves. Case in point, he is wrong.

This example might be brutal to swallow, but such is life. You take the good with the bad and carry on. Life is sunshine and rain. When the sun is shining, smile and enjoy. When life brings rain, smile and enjoy the lesson.

Let's use another typical example, that of being fired from a job. Now, remember the 99-to-1 rule we discussed prior, as this, along with the example of a man being left by a mate and it being a surprise to him, is applicable and relevant. We're talking 99% here—always unless specified otherwise.

Think back on a situation that was tough for you when you were let go. Think back to the time you were with a company, think back to all the things you know you did wrong or could have done better while you were there and thought no one knew or no one was looking. When the universe was looking, you were looking and possibly your boss or coworkers too.

Remember, as the Bible says, "We reap what we sow." What goes around comes around; what you put out will come back; what you give is what you get. This is called "karma." It's real and even more powerful than many credit until they start to believe in the power of the universe and their own power. And when karma hits, it hits hard. It wasn't your boss who didn't like you or Karen in the office who would constantly stir up drama. It was you all along, and you now know just how wrong you were. And the best part about this is that it's okay to be wrong. The sooner you accept this, the sooner you'll be free.

Next, we'll discuss the learning process after the mistake has been made. This is the golden key to learn how to turn a mistake into an opportunity to learn and grow.

THE THIRD STEP TO BEING WRONG:
WHAT DID I LEARN? (THE LESSON)

Once we're okay with the idea of being wrong, accepting that being wrong is just a part of our day, we can then open ourselves up to learn how not to make those mistakes again. We learn the lesson to save time in the future from continually making the same mistakes.

Let's go back to the example of being let go from a job. Now that you've accepted that it's okay, you can learn that it's likely your fault you were let go. The silver lining is finding the lesson that won't yield the same result for the next job.

When you take the time to self-reflect, not only on yourself but the situations you've been a part of, you can find room for improvement to do better. When it comes to being let go from a job, as tough as the news can be, that's the very opportunity to ask yourself where you can improve, not only as an employee but also as a person.

Let's say you know you came to work, showed up, did your job, and then went home daily for three years. You expected a raise because you've been there for a year and know raises can be handed out annually. So: You show up, rinse, wash, repeat.

Maybe you plan for the weekend because you work a typical 9–5 job. You don't have to work on the weekends and that's precisely what your mind is focused on. What are the plans for the weekend? You're 25 years old and COVID isn't in effect, so you can go out with your friends and party Friday night. All week, you're looking forward to Friday night. Maybe subconsciously you're not giving your focus to your work, projects, team members and boss because you know that special someone will be in the group of friends at the bar.

Then, once Friday night comes and goes, you're hung over. Saturday, you either don't drink or drink a little to rest up for Sunday fun day. Sunday comes, you get drunk again and boom, your alarm goes off Monday morning at 6:00 am. You dread getting out of bed, but you know in the back of your mind, the weekend is only four days and a wake-up away.

After a long commute, you get to work, hung over and tired, pour that third cup of coffee and try to focus, but damn, Sunday was so good, you tell stories about it to your coworkers. You finish what you need to, and then leave for the day. Tuesday rolls around, and you're still a bit hung over whether you know it or not, and show up to work, maybe getting a little more done than the previous day.

Wednesday comes around, and you actually accomplish your goal for the day of the week because you're no longer hung over. Still, you know Friday is right around the corner. Thursday, you get some work done but know the crew is meeting tomorrow night, so when you show up to work on Friday, you're not getting much done. You're ready for the weekend.

THE LESSON

Some of you reading these words might not have thought about this situation in this manner or lens of focus before. The reality is setting in that your being let go from that job was, in fact, your fault. Not your boss, manager, coworkers, husband, boyfriend, girlfriend, gender-neutral friend, best friend, mom, dad, sister, brother, pet, dog, cat, the news: It was your fault all along, no matter the excuse you fabricate to have felt differently in the moment.

When you look at what you could have done better while at the job, it's simple. The priorities you have say a lot about you as a human. If partying for the weekend is the importance, that's low-hanging fruit and an easy fix.

Sleeping well, exercising, being a good human, meditation, gratitude journaling and working harder instead of just showing up—going above and beyond at work, let alone with life, doing more than you have to do, doing what needs to be done to better yourself and everyone around you is a priority to adapt, especially if you want to be a high earner in life.

It's a simple fix; it's challenging to do the right thing, at first anyway, as you're breaking your old, dated priorities and behaviors. With time, doing the right thing, going above and beyond will become natural and easy. There's a saying, "Do more than you're paid, and soon you'll be paid for more than you do."

Here's a great show about how to reinforce these principles, where I walk you through how to get a $30,000 a year raise. Go to *chriswarnes.com* and select the podcast tab, Episode 32: "How to Increase Your Pay."

When I was a teenager, I worked at my local Dunkin Donuts and was fired by a family friend for selling my friend's food at a discounted price. I was angry and blamed the boss for my lack of work and having no money.

As time went on, I reflected on this situation and found I was wrong all along. It took stepping aside from the problem to realize I was the one in the wrong, not the boss.

The sooner you step aside from your emotions, think about

the situation objectively, self-reflect and look for the opportunity within the lesson, the sooner you'll free yourself from feeling guilt or the embracement of being wrong. When you're free from the feeling of being wrong, you'll learn how to never make that mistake again. When you know how to not make mundane mistakes, you save yourself heartache, problems, sleepless nights, money and most importantly, time.

THE FOURTH STEP TO BEING WRONG: HOW TO NEVER MAKE THIS MISTAKE AGAIN

Now that we've covered how great mistakes actually are, first by being okay with making mistakes, second by identifying the mistake and third, learning from it, the key now is to move to the final phase of building your action plan to not make a mistake again. This is the most critical stage and maybe the stage you struggle with most when taking responsibility for your actions and being okay with your mistakes.

Once we get this far, we try to problem-solve how not to make a mistake again. However, with more significant mistakes, it might take the practice of these action plans as they may not work from the start. That's okay, as big problems need a lot of attention and have "working action plans" that need adjusting given the context.

Let's use the idea of being pulled over for speeding as a simple example of a mistake and rectifying it. You're okay with this mistake even if it's expensive. Second, you understand you can't go 40 mph in a 25mph school zone. Third, you learn this will cost you $300, and you don't want to make this mistake again.

Moving into the fourth phase, it's simple: no more speeding, let alone in a 25mph school zone. Suppose we use a higher-level example, such as being terminated from your job. You may have to dive deeper on the fourth step to uncover the lesson, so you'll never be fired again. It will take self-reflecting and being honest with yourself to discover your plan to not make a mistake also may not have worked.

The higher the level of a problem, the more complex the

action plan can be to not make a repeated mistake. Vice versa, the smaller or easier the mistake, the easier the action plan, and the likelihood of the mistake not happening again will be high.

No matter what, the growth you want out of life, all you desire, everything you want stands on the other side of you, looking at the mirror, pointing the finger inward and being okay with the fact that you're not and won't ever be perfect. You will make mistakes and are now open-minded enough to grow into the person you've always desired. The first step is accepting your BS and mistakes as okay.

Now, we move into setting up your morning and harnessing your purest daily energy with the blueprint of a highly effective morning routine.

CHAPTER 3

YOUR MORNING ROUTINE

I knew of the concept of having a morning routine for many years before putting it into motion. I think to myself, if I'd only started when I first heard about the idea, how advanced my mindset would be, along with my understanding of the universe and its laws.

When we learn to harness our purest, most transparent energy—our morning energy—we embark on a journey to not only enlighten our minds, free our minds, learn our minds, but also heal our minds. Healing is the reason I took the plunge and started with morning routines because I'd learned that meditation could reverse, revert and potentially rid me of trauma...in my case from PTSD. I'd been diagnosed with PSTD upon leaving the Army after two combat tours in Iraq. I was fascinated that I could change my brain by learning to meditate, working to undo heavy trauma that was deep-rooted by war.

Our minds are superhighways of thoughts, energy and ideas flying back and forth and spreading through the body. When the mind has trauma, the highway has a huge roadblock that holds information, not allowing it to pass. Meditation is known to knock down these roadblocks and walls, freeing the information, thoughts, vibes so the energy no longer sticks, allowing ideas to have new highways and paths. Once I decided to do the work of facing myself, the demons, shadows, the darkness, the shortcoming and the one dream that haunted me daily for nearly a decade post-war, I began to free my mind, in turn freeing myself from myself.

As you've learned if you've started this practice to rid your-self of traumas—or will be on your journey of ridding yourself after learning this lesson—it will be demanding from the start.

You might want to quit, as it can be challenging to face yourself; however, I assure you the light at the end of the tunnel shining down upon your face once you've put in the inner work is more than worth the initial discomforts faced at the beginning of the journey.

Push past the pain. Kick the beehive—get stung by those bees and soon you'll smile, proud of how far you've come.

A morning routine is something that, once learned, might change your life. We take some time in the morning, waking up earlier—which should be complemented by going to bed earlier by shutting off the TV, Netflix or not going out.

When everything will change is when you're proactive in thinking about needed sleep, prioritizing the time allotted to build and execute your morning routine. You'll have an epiph-any that a TV show doesn't matter, nor do your drunk friends at the bar complaining about life, but what does matter is the time you dedicate to harnessing that pure energy every morning before everyone else wakes up.

Get out of bed like you're on a mission to change the world. Leave your phone off, find a quiet and comfortable place and focus on filling up your glass so you can pour from it during the day into situations and people who need your attention and energy. This isn't a selfish practice. This is a *selfless* practice to take an hour for yourself or longer to be at your best operating ability by taking care of yourself to optimally affect everyone else in your life.

It may be that your family, friends, coworkers, team or em-ployees will notice the change and want to know what you're do-ing and why. Don't expect them to mirror what you do, though. We can only hold the door open for others; they have to walk through it. If they want the inner peace bad enough, they will.

Now, let's get to it. These ideas don't have to be done in the order written. In fact, I encourage you to play with the order of each in your morning routine and see what works best for you. We're all different and prefer a different sequence.

I often get asked which order to perform these and how long to do each exercise. The answer is precisely the same when I'm asked to describe the best diet: There's no single best diet other than the one that works for you.

As for timing, I recommend starting with an hour, if not more. That means using a timer, reading for 15 minutes, gratitude journaling, meditating for 15 minutes and writing affirmations for 15 minutes each.

There's no right or wrong when it comes to morning routines. However, this practice is to be done in the morning. This is only what I suggest because it's worked wonders for me. I now open the door for you, but it's you who must walk through.

Here is a mock one-hour routine format, and we'll get in depth with each piece of the routine later in the chapter. If you can only allot 30 minutes to your morning routine due to life obligations, adjust the timing to fit your needs.

5:00 a.m.—*Read something uplifting or empowering. Any book or article on self-development will do. However, it isn't limited to self-development.*

5:15 a.m.—*Gratitude journal. Write about all you're thankful and grateful for, while also writing what you desire. I'll discuss this in depth later in the chapter.*

5:30 a.m.—*Meditation.*

5:45 a.m.—*Write and then speak aloud your affirmations, speaking into existence what you're affirming. We'll cover the details of affirmations later in the chapter.*

6:00 a.m.—*Done. Now you're ready to tackle your day and help everyone in your life as your cup is now full for pouring.*

Let's discuss.

READ YOUR WAY TO KNOWLEDGE

Growing up, you couldn't get me to read a book. There was no way. Teachers could assign a reading assignment to read and write a report on. They could tell me there was a test on a book —really, anything they wanted to throw at me. I did not read an entire book from high school to my first attempt at college in 2003, failing out at Southern Connecticut State University with a GPA of .73 after only two semesters.

That landed me in the Army in 2004.

The turning point was heavy; when my life and the lives of people around me depended on the knowledge I was required to read, it flipped a switch, and I began reading the assigned military doctrine.

After separating from the military in 2009, I reentered school. I once again read what was required of me, primarily studying history, exercise science, nutrition and business. Reading for fun or with the lens on developing my mind was missing.

Somewhere around 2013, I decided I needed to know more on topics I found interesting. That started with how some combat veterans could return home and make something big of themselves, freeing themselves from their experienced trauma.

I began with Marcus Luttrell's *Lone Survivor* and Chris Kyle's *American Sniper*. Both books—and men—are great examples of heavy hitters who came home to fight their own battles and build their brands by telling mind-blowing stories. They served together in one of the most elite fighting forces to ever walk the earth: the United States Navy SEALs.

That sparked me to want to learn more about success, leadership, team building, psychology, money, customer service and entrepreneurship, so I started with one of the best books ever written by my favorite author and arguably one of the best humans to ever live: *How to Win Friends and Influence People* by Dale Carnegie. That book singlehandedly started my development journey, which built and compounded, opening up doors I never knew existed.

Now let's get into selecting your reading list and discuss

how to schedule reading in your morning routine.

The key to reading for a high performer or if you aspire to be one is to schedule your reading times or the amount you plan to read. The excuse I hear most often is, "I don't have time to read." When you decide you'd rather die than not take a single step forward, you decide to complete everything at hand.

"A coach is someone who tells you what you don't want to hear, who helps you see what you don't want to see so you can be who you've always known you could be."
~ Tom Landry

Reading was the first piece of a morning routine I put into practice many years ago. I had to schedule it by physically writing into my schedule to read first thing in the morning. That's what it took to push past the excuses holding comfort in my life. I'd wake up between 5–6:00 a.m. and brew my coffee. When I sat to drink my coffee, I'd also read. I'd read a painful 10 pages, taking anywhere from 20–30 minutes.

Start with whatever you can comfortably do. It may be five pages, 10 pages, 30 minutes or an hour as I commonly do, especially if it's a topic or author I love. No matter what, no matter the timeframe you have to work with, reading will help you improve your vocabulary, grammar, spelling and knowledge base. Use a pen or highlighter to mark what sticks out.

I also often go back and review the content that speaks to me. When rereading books, you'll read them differently because your life has progressed, along with your perspective. I often use a different color pen when rereading books to display how those books speak to me as time moves on.

There's no right or wrong order to perform your morning routine. At times, you may want to meditate or pray first and that's okay. Do whatever feels is best for you or what your mind is nudging you to do.

If you wake up and feel the calling to read first, try it; see how it works and shift it in your morning routine schedule as needed. Just do it rather than skipping it. Grow your mind, your knowledge, your vocabulary. Grow yourself and you won't recognize yourself as you develop the most powerful tool mankind was blessed with, your mind.

Pro tip: Once you've been reading for a bit and have discovered the books you love, read them annually. Find a core group of books you love and study them annually. For example, I've read Carnegie's *How to Win Friends and Influence People* annually for many years, and it has helped tremendously.

GRATITUDE

This section might be life-changing. Each topic we discuss is a topic that can greatly impact your life, changing your life significantly at different points. Gratitude is commonly overlooked as we find ourselves caught up in everything other than actually being grateful for the things we have and that happen to us. Open YouTube and search "Chris Warnes Gratitude" for more commentary on this.

There were a couple points in my life when gratitude stuck out and resonated deeply with the compelling soul-changing presence effect it had on me: war and closing my largest business. Both situations stripped me to my core and put in front of me what was most important: family, friends, pets, a roof over my head, a pillow under my head, food to eat, running water and all the meaningful and even meaningless material things I'd collected.

Gratitude is something we have to find on our own. It can't be given as a present to understand. It can't be bought on Amazon; it can't be paid for—it has to be uncovered from within. From the depth of our hearts, we must discover what means the most to us.

You might have to search the depths of your soul, the depths of your heart, the depth of your being before you find what it is you're grateful for, but once you find it, your world as you know it will change for the better.

What I'm grateful for will differ from what you're grateful

for. However, once we understand the strength found in harnessing gratitude, we can find it in all walks of life, in all dealings through the day, everywhere we look if we train ourselves to see it. And when you teach yourself to stop, look around and appreciate all that you have, what you're surrounded by, you have trained yourself to enjoy life and have gratitude for living.

Even if you don't understand gratitude, there's a practice of writing about gratitude that will not only speed up the process of understanding, but also rewrite your mind, thoughts and beliefs on the subject.

This practice, which is used by many, is called "gratitude journaling" and is a process done daily to rewrite the subconscious mind to look for and feel gratitude. I use this practice to wholeheartedly feel gratitude throughout the day. It gives me a new meaning of being thankful as my skin sometimes tightens and welts for minutes as I feel the energy of gratitude.

To read a complete story about how to appreciate your life, being grateful for it, but if the idea of gratitude is foreign to you, I recommend reading a book that will shake you to your soul, driving home how every single day is an absolute blessing: *Man's Search for Meaning* by Viktor E. Frankl.

Frankl's account of being pulled from his life and forced to become not a human but a living number in the infamous kill camps, better known as concentration camps, notably the infamous Auschwitz during the height of the Nazi German terror in the early 1940s during World War II. A man like me, who has seen the horrors of war, can wholeheartedly say this book is a book that can put into perspective not only gratitude, but also how great we all have it living in a time as progressive as we do nearly 80 years post-World War II.

Let's consider the process of journaling to reinforce gratitude, with one of the best practices I learned along the way: gratitude journaling.

GRATITUDE JOURNAL

Find yourself a nice notebook and a favorite pen. We're

using pen and paper here, not phones or computers, because handwriting is critical for programming and encoding new information into the subconscious mind. Get a big notebook because if you're anything like me, you'll need to write a lot to undo or rewrite years of false beliefs, choices and patterns.

When you write your daily gratitude letter, report your words to anyone you want: yourself, higher self, God, source, the universe, ancestors, angels, passed family members…anyone really. I write to my dad and the universe as I'm a believer in not only the universe, but that we're all connected by energy.

There is no right or wrong in whom you write to. Just write to someone you feel is worthy of hearing what you're grateful for, along with what you'll be thankful for, the things to come in your life. Think of and then write, expressing gratitude for what you already have, such as a loving family or spouse, amazing pet, a roof over your head, food to eat, clothing to wear and so on, but not limited to.

Here's a favorite quote to help drive the point home:

*"I cried because I had no shoes
until I met a man who had no feet."*
~ Helen Keller

And then think about and write expressing gratitude for all you'd like to receive as though you've received it. Write in the present tense. This is a perfect opportunity to list goals you want to achieve, such as reaching better health, higher income, promotion, relationships, anything material, and isn't limited to anything written.

I encourage you to think deeply about all you want; nothing you want is too big or out of reach. If you want a one-billion-dollar empire, good, write it and begin the process of manifesting your dreams through gratitude journaling.

You'll write your gratitude in solid words that will bring forth emotion. You'll begin to feel what you're writing and saying—I'll talk later in the book about speaking whatever you desire into existence.

Always remember, the key is to express as though you've already manifested these goals into your life, writing and speaking in the present tense.

"Your arms wide open, the walls are caving in
Don't bury your secrets deep within your skin
When you focus on the good things
All things under the sun
You free yourself from negativity
And then the good shall come"
~ Stick Figure

(From Choice is Yours, used with permission)

GRATITUDE JOURNAL EXAMPLE

This is an example of what works for me and my students. Feel free to use it as your blueprint while beginning to gratitude journal. The key is to understand the principles written and transfer the ideas that relate to you and your life. Interject your goals into your own gratitude journal. Make the journal yours.

"Dear Dad and Spirit (again, write to whom you feel compelled to write). I come to you this morning with a heart full of love, joy and gratitude for you in my life, for hearing me and supporting me always no matter what, as you're my partner in life and business. I'm grateful for you eternally as you're the ever-powerful source of my unlimited supply. Thank you so much for all I have, for my warm home, a great night's sleep, food to eat, continued health, the excellent relationships in my life.

"All that's in my life is for my highest and best good. May all others find their good elsewhere, be happy and free. I'm so thankful for all I have and am continuing to be blessed with, my growing and wildly profitable companies where I can touch millions of lives, helping others understand they too have the capacity, power and ability to create what life they desire.

"I'm the best mentor and best business coach to ever live. My course and systems continue to change lives, and I'm a worldwide best-selling author with gratitude at the forefront of my thinking. I'm supplied with a plan and when this plan is received, I'll follow it tirelessly.

"Thank you for (insert financial income goal) that came to my life and blessed me with the ability to help and teach countless more humans to discover their power to live a life full of purpose of the highest power. Thank you for the long and healthy life of my number one angel, my dog Penelope, and may she live a long, happy, healthy and fulfilled life for many years to come.

"Thank you for all the lessons I've learned that brought me closer to my soul mate so we can share a beautiful, long-lasting love and life together. I give up and trust. I give up and trust. I give up and trust that you supply me with all I'm divinely in alignment with. There's gold in the air and I'm a money magnet. May these words be done and free to the law and power of the universe."

Love, CW

The power of a gratitude letter is something I encourage you to experience in your life. If you're looking to understand the subject of gratitude journaling thoroughly, I encourage you to read *The Path To Wealth* if you're an entrepreneur, or if not an entrepreneur, read *The Gratitude Formula*. These are both by May McCarthy, a nine-figure entrepreneur, powerhouse and a serious proponent of spirituality and how to harness financial freedom through principles of the Law of Attraction.

MEDITATION

I can write about many forms of meditation to teach the art of meditation, but just know that if you've never meditated, it might not be easy from the start. Your mind will wander aimlessly or more than likely anyway. That's normal for beginners, and even with seasoned meditators. The key to meditation is to control your mind and the thoughts racing through it, which is how we learn mindfulness.

For beginners, I recommend guided meditations—recorded tracks of vocal, vocal and music or just beats (not limited to only these, but they're the most common). There are great apps like Headspace that can custom build to your likes and dislikes. Google "guided meditation," pulling up YouTube to listen to what catches your eye.

Guided meditations are great. They tell you what to think about, how to breathe and feel, allowing newbies to let go and start meditating. Some work well for my students in Warrior Consulting; I especially like gratitude, forgiveness, prosperity, abundance and breathing meditations. These prompts or topics are the biggest hits. Some of the best-guided meditations are written by Bob Proctor and Esther (Abraham) Hicks.

SETTING A PROPER ENVIRONMENT

Find a pleasant and comfortable area of your home that's dark and where you're alone, quiet and peaceful. This will ensure a perfect environment to meditate. Similar to sleeping well, you must set your environment for proper meditation.

Let's start with a sleep environment concept to foreshadow how important it is to control your environment—in this case, a morning routine environment. Many people don't know how important sleep is to the body, and if that's you, I'm here to help educate you.

Once separating from the military, I became a personal trainer and found success because my military-style went over well. I learned that exercise is excellent and nutrition even more so, but mindset and sleep are the two that turn the tables of a fitness lifestyle. Rest and the environment you set are where you make your money hitting REM cycles. REM, or rapid eye movement, happens every 90 minutes and is responsible for many things, including HGH or human growth hormone release, which is what repairs and heals your body.

Hitting several REM cycles through the night might seem like a fundamental idea to some, but appears to elude most

Americans, given our state of physical and mental health.

We're the 10th most overweight and most heavily medicated country in the history of the world, which can be traced back to a simple concept of the quality of our sleep. Getting great sleep starts with your bedtime routine.

As ironic as it may seem, you're beginning to realize that the quality of your morning routine is correlated with your evening routine. One of the biggest keys is to take your eyes off screens that emit blue light 60 to 90 minutes before bed.

Modern phones and tablets have caught on to this concept and have "night modes" that limit blue light emission, but it's best to put away all screens, phones, iPads, tablets, iWatch, computers and TVs. Reading, stretching and foam rolling are a few activities I recommend during an evening routine, along with connecting with your partner, having sex or even talking on the phone.

Later in the chapter, we'll outline how to properly execute your evening routine.

"Close your eyes for a moment
Focus on the air that you breathe
Think good thoughts, and now hold them
Now you slip into a dream
And now you slip away to another place
Above the storms and rain
You're miles away, you're miles away
Said if you're just now waking up
I want to send you all some love"
~ Stick Figure
(From Above the Storm, used with permission)

Let's get back to the morning routine and meditation environment. Find a dark, quiet and peaceful space, seated or lying, where you can be alone with your mindfulness and thoughts. Load your favorite guided meditation and shut your eyes. Listen to the meditation and follow all instructions.

When your mind wanders off, which will happen, zero in

on the fact that you're wandering and refocus, listening again to the guided meditation instructions. There's no "best" time frame, but five or ten minutes to start is ideal for a beginner.

As you advance and get better at meditating, you can increase your time, spending up to an hour or more meditating if you have the bandwidth. I find anywhere between five and 25 minutes is the perfect time, depending on my wants, needs, schedule and mood. Twenty minutes isn't easy, especially for beginners. Meditation is an art of mindfulness and it will take time to get better. With practice you *will* get better.

After you feel you've done well with guided meditations, I want you to try visualization meditations. Many like to do both during the day or move between the two types of meditations depending on the day.

Let's look at the definition of visualization to best understand. "When you visualize, you focus on something specific— an event, person or goal you want to achieve—and hold it in your mind, imagining your outcome becoming a reality," as per Healthline. You can find more at healthline.com/health/visualization-meditation.

Visualization is a mindfulness technique of its own, but you can also use it to enhance regular meditation. Adding visualization to your meditation mix allows you to better direct your relaxed mind toward specific outcomes you'd like to see in your life.

Again from *healthline.com:* "Visualization is also linked to potential health benefits such as increased athletic performance, relief of anxiety and depression symptoms, improved relaxation, greater compassion for yourself and others, empathy, pain relief, improved ability to cope with stress, improved sleep, better emotional and physical wellness and increased self-control."

Things I want to manifest in life, from partners, employees, books, system and course launches, cars, money amounts, health and so on are great topics to shut my eyes and visualize. I recommend the same to you.

Free your mind through meditation today.

AN EXAMPLE OF A VISION YOU CAN CREATE

You're the architect of your visions and visualization practices. You can create any vision you want, as the more you do so, the more likely what you see on the screen of your mind will be held in your hand. There's no limit to what you can visualize or create; ANYTHING you desire you can have.

Here's a macro vision of mine—I'll discuss a micro idea later in this chapter—building what I want life to look like, as you can too. Many years ago, I had a different macro vision of what my life would look like, and much of it I am or have lived since, to include opening, building and running businesses, revenue amounts, cars in my driveway, delivering services to customers, dating partners that fit my wants, high-end clothing along with beautiful timepieces I loved. These are just a few examples of what I built into my visions and manifested into reality, as you can too, with practice and dedication.

Now, I have an abnormally clear vision of my life. The detail is striking, from the color of the car, shifting gears and holding the steering wheel, hearing the engine scream, to the color of the kitchen cabinets and marble countertops, down to the swirl in the marble, the outdoor patio, the texture of the stone under my feet, the temperature of the pool water I'm swimming in—and yes, my skin tightens up when visioning myself swimming in my beautiful pool with its cold water. The key is to develop your vision down to the exact detail of what you desire: think it, feel it and live it.

I usually start with the end of my legacy in my vision: closing the fifth book, my autobiography. I'm seated in a study located off a master walk-in closet, surrounded by a library of the books I've read over the years. I'm sitting on a beautiful leather chair. Adjacent to a matching chair is a black and white marble chess board.

I close the book and walk into my closet that's filled with beautiful items, to include my favorite outfits, which are chinos, loafers, button-down, fine sports jackets and of course, matching pocket squares that pop big time and command presence and respect. As I put on my outfit, I walk out of my closet to my master bedroom with my partner lying in bed to greet me and ensure I look perfect. My dogs lick me until I can no longer take it and I'm smiling ear to ear.

I make my way down my staircase to see my closest friends and their families on the far side of my kitchen, my staff, team and their families running around. My mother is cooking for all of us. I hand her a bag of cash and then see my friends playing pool on my table and, of course, break my stones for looking like a male model.

As I make my way outside, I head in one of two directions, either the garage or my backyard pool. For the sake of the vision, we'll head to the garage, with six bays, full of five of my dream cars, and the last bay has pallets of my books. I pick whichever car I'm in the mood for and head off for the day.

I usually have a shipment of many products with me for my customers. I stop by FedEx and send them, packaged with a handwritten card, a signature of mine used in business for more than a decade. I then have a split in the road where I either head to my yacht, where my friends and team have gotten ready for me or to the jet.

We'll head to the plane, where I'm met by my closest team members and dogs. I have a performance waiting for me at our destination. Once I get there, I speak on a stage with other greats in the personal development field or at Washington, DC, speaking where Martin Luther King Jr. did.

I deliver my performance and am then signing and handing out books to eager fans to meet me and take pictures. My team and dogs are with me, always protecting me and helping with anything I need. Once I exit, I head back to the jet with my people and then get back to my home airport, cars waiting and head back home to sit down and reread my legacy.

This is an example of a vision I've built and shared with you. You can create any vision you desire too. And in turn, you'll manifest all you want into your life, as I have and continue to work on building.

As we close out the discussion on meditations, I'll now

guide you through how to schedule your time as a student of life. Remember, there's no right or wrong way of doing your morning routine. The key is finding the process, order, and pieces that work best for you. You'll now read an example of what works best for me and my students, which is ever-evolving as we learn more daily.

You can and will take control of your life, starting with your mornings. All you desire can be accomplished. All you dream of will manifest.

THE DAILY ROUTINE

Before we move on, let's unpack the success of your morning routine and how it all starts with the prior evening and the evening routine you'll inevitably adopt because you know it's essential. Winding down from the day is important for your well-being, health and the sleep to come.

If you're interested in a great book that goes into detail about how to sleep ideally, I'd highly recommend Shawn Stevenson's *Sleep Smarter*. He does a fantastic job describing precisely what humans need to do to rest well, using his story of healing his body as a once high-performing athlete, to a tragic injury and back to top-tier athlete by harnessing the power of sleep.

Let's use a bedtime of 9:00 p.m. since we're also using the wake-up time of 5:00 a.m. I'm not directing you to go to bed at 9:00 p.m. and wake up at 5:00 a.m., as your needs may be different after working third shift or even overnight. These are just templates we're using to understand the timing and how to optimize your sleep as an example.

Now, since our bedtime in this example is 9:00 p.m., at 7:30 p.m. you'll shut off all screens, including phones, TVs, iPad, tablets, computers and any other screen you own. This will drastically decrease the emitted blue lights picked up by your eyes. Those blue lights keep our minds running at night when we try to fall asleep and worse, they keep us out of REM cycles while sleeping.

PREPARING TO DOMINATE THE DAY TO COME

The 90 minutes of no screens can be used to accomplish whatever you desire; however, we'll discuss some activities I've found have helped not only me, but also many students and clients I've worked with to prepare for a long, restful and deep sleep.

When I was an up-and-coming businessman, I picked up some tips from successful businessmen further along than me when they'd discuss being prepared for the day to come. With this advice, I molded it to my needs, which were at the time and still are similar.

I enjoy living in a clean home; I'll wash dishes to keep a clean sink overnight, prepare my coffee to perk before rising in the morning, meal prepping for the day to come, having all my meals and food ready to go to just grab and go the following day, along with laying out my outfit for the next day and also my gym gear and packing my gym bag, easily accessible to be loaded in the car the following morning.

Let's call this portion of the evening routine "preparing to dominate the day to come." There are many more activities you can do, like laundry, cleaning up the home and walking the dog. Get yourself ready for the morning to come, when you have less to do, can think about less and make decisions early in the morning. This significantly helps conserve time as you begin to condition yourself to waking up earlier to accomplish the morning routine.

LIGHT ACTIVITY

Now that you're ready to crush the day to come, let's shift focus to your body and preparing the body to sleep. I'm a massive enthusiast of daily soft-tissue fascia release such as foam rolling and stretching.

Suppose you exercise rigorously and enjoy a healthy lifestyle. In that case, you must be proactive in taking care of your body by foam rolling and stretching daily to avoid catching serious injuries, increasing blood flow, range of motion, mobility and flexibility.

Foam rolling and stretching should be centered around workout time and also before bed to help your mind and body start the ease into sleep mode, encouraging the shift from cortisol production, which is the daytime running hormone, to melatonin, the evening hormone. I recommend foam rolling for 5–10 minutes, rolling your whole body with a focus on the muscle group or groups recently trained or that are sore.

Once you've rolled, do static or dynamic stretches for 5–10 minutes over your whole body, with a focus on muscle groups or groups recently exercised or that are sore.

Take care of your body and your body will take care of you. It's that simple. This can also be a time to perform yoga or walk the dog. Wind down and lightly move your body. This practice will help you relax quickly and should be a staple in everyone's evening routine.

MOVING TO THE BEDROOM

Now that you're ready to crush the day and morning to come, your body is relaxed and stretched. If you're not already in the bedroom, it's time to move there. The bedroom is only for two activities to create a proper sleeping environment. Therefore, remove all screens, TV and phones if you're serious about getting great rest. The bedroom isn't for eating, watching TV… and so on. It's for sleep and sex—that's all—to create the energy needed to have the optimal environment for sleeping.

This can be a great time to spend with your partner, if you have one, talking, listening to one another, being present with no phones or TV to distract you. Massaging one another and, of course, sleeping with each other. With the intent not to stray too far from the topic of the evening routine, not only will having sex with your partner before bed help you sleep better, but if you're in a relationship, there must be a healthy sexual aspect of your connection to keep a harmonious relationship intact.

Suppose you and your partner have moved away from sleeping with one another. This is your chance to change your choices to find it again because not only will your sleep improve, so will your relationship and your life.

SPOKEN AFFIRMATIONS

There are two specific topics you can think about, visualize, write or speak before bed that will drastically help center you and your energy before drifting off to sleep.

Forgiveness and gratitude are the two topics that land deeply for many, to include me. In the next chapter, we'll dive into detail explaining forgiveness affirmations.

We've already touched upon gratitude, but I'll lay out how to quickly speak aloud, affirming both forgiveness and gratitude. While lying in bed or in a quiet place before bed, think about everything you're grateful for that day and speak your thanks out loud.

Maybe you met a significant lead, closed a big sale, a friend helped you with a project, you passed a test or are just grateful to be alive. Speak it out loud and feel it, smile while affirming and vibrate gratitude. This will help you sleep peacefully and wake up refreshed and ready to go like someone on a mission to change the world.

Here's an example:

"Thank you, _____ (insert who you pray to) for the fantastic lead you blessed me with today. Thank you for the massive sale of _____ (insert amount) to help grow our business and bless me with continued wealth. Thank you for the help from_____ (insert name of friend). I'm full of gratitude to be alive and well today. Thank you."

It's pretty simple to be thankful, focus on the small things, and then your focus will grow. A great tip I learned is to carry around a small 3x3 notebook to jot down all the great I experience through the day to reference when needing a reminder of the great I've been manifesting.

With forgiveness, think about anyone who could use your forgiveness. Ideally, as time goes on, you'll think about people in your life you'd like to forgive, releasing them to find their good elsewhere and, in turn, forgiving you.

A tremendous verbal affirmation I learned from May Mc-

Carthy goes like this:

> *"Dear divine true self of* _____
> *(insert your name or another person you want to forgive),*
> *I bless you; I love you; I forgive you; I release you."*

You might find only a few people pop into mind or you may have dozens. There's no right or wrong way of speaking forgiveness as long as you mean it and truthfully feel and want to forgive others, creating room for more good to come your way.

PURPOSE DEGREE

While we haven't spoken much on the subject of purpose in this book, purpose is your guiding light, the map to your world and is what you're obsessed with to create your life around fulfillment. It's why you're here in this life.

Of many well-written authors, Napoleon Hill is the best on the topic of purpose. He articulates how to understand purpose, and gets the gears in motion to understand your purpose.

> *"It's most appalling to know that 95 percent of the people of the world are drifting aimlessly through life, without the slightest concept of the work for which they're best fitted and with no conception whatsoever of even the need of such a thing as a defined objective toward which to strive."*
> **~ Napoleon Hill,** *Laws of Success*

Napoleon says, "Any definite purpose that is deliberately fixed in the mind and held there, with the determination to realize it, finally saturates the entire subconscious mind until it automatically influences the physical action of the body toward the attainment of that purpose."

When the time comes to select your purpose in life, think about what you do best. Consider something you can do better than anyone else and then organize your thinking around believing you're here in this life to execute that purpose. For example, my purpose in life is to teach humans they can live the life they dream of. I tell myself this often throughout the day, always before I fall asleep at night and as soon as I rise in the morning.

I encourage you to put thought into your defined purpose,

then verbally affirm it out loud before falling asleep at night to plant the seed of what you're here for, watering that seed nightly and then firming the belief with concrete by repetition.

MOCK EVENING ROUTINE WITH TIMELINES

Here's an evening routine anyone can use. Play with the order along with the actual times to best suit your needs.

7:30 p.m.—*All screens are turned off and put away, including your phone*

7:45 p.m.—*Clean up and prepare for the day to come*

8:15 p.m.—*Do light physical activities such as stretching, yoga or foam rolling*

8:30 p.m.—*Bed and partner time*

9:00 p.m.—*Verbal affirmations and purpose degree*

9:05 p.m.–5:00 a.m.—*Sleep well, sleep deeply, hitting your REM cycles, waking up ready to take on the world*

CHAPTER 4

AFFIRMATIONS

There was a time when I'd teach affirmations in the morning routine chapter or module while coaching group courses. However, as time has gone on, I've come to a conclusion through application and understanding many humans I've taught over the years that the subject of affirmations is best taught separate from the morning routine. Affirmations can be added to your morning routine because there's no right or wrong way to execute your morning or self-development routine.

Actually, I encourage you to add affirmations to your morning routine. I'm only providing you with an open door to walk through in freeing yourself from yourself by ultimately facing who you see in the mirror and moving past the preprogrammed beliefs we all have that hold us back. Personally, I've found affirmations make for a great addition to my morning routine or other situational points during the day. I learned the power of affirmations from greats in the Law of Attraction field such as May McCarthy with her book *The Path to Wealth,* Catherine Ponder in her notable book *The Dynamic Laws of Prosperity,* Bob Proctor, Abraham Hicks and, of course, the great Napoleon Hill in several of his books, to include *Think and Grow Rich* along with *The Law of Success.*

Let's take a look at the definition of the word "affirmation" before we move on. "In New Thought and New Age, terminology refer primarily to the practice of positive thinking and self-empowerment—fostering a belief that a positive mental attitude supported by affirmations will achieve success

in anything. More specifically, affirmation is a carefully format-
ted statement that should be repeated to one's self and written
down frequently. For affirmations to be effective, it's said that
they need to be present tense, positive, personal and specific."

~Per https://en.wikipedia.org/wiki/Affirmations_(New_Age)

As children growing up, we don't know right from wrong,
as our choices are given to us by those who raise us. We're told,
taught and shown what to believe and that formulates our op-
tions and beliefs as we grow.

Church and religion are examples of a belief that's forced
on many by parents. I was forced to go to church weekly, along
with catechism, also known as Sunday School. My mother
thought our family should embrace the word of God and I was
raised, baptized and confirmed Roman Catholic, which is a big
deal having Italian heritage. This was the environment I was
provided and a choice that wasn't mine, much like you may be
able to relate—an example of a choice that wasn't ours and that
we thought was normal, playing a part in our beliefs and subconscious programming.

Your subconscious is written by what you're taught, what
you were provided by the environment in which you grew up,
and what guides 95 percent of your conscious decision-making.
Staggering statistics, right? I thought so too, when I first learned
it. Of course, you might find articles that propose less than 95
percent; however, that point is that your subconscious mind is
your guiding compass to everything you think and do in life, all
rooted in your early environment.

Before I teach you how to rewrite your belief system as
you discover you want more or better from life and are ready
to pursue that, let me tell you about a student of mine, LJ. LJ
came to me knowing he had more to offer but was stuck, much
like the rest of us, including students who find me to help them
understand themselves, their blocks and to learn how to move
past them.

Much like most humans, LJ had confidence issues due to a
toxic environment growing up with domineering and masculine

mother who continually belittled and suppressed the male family members, including him, for the first 30 years of his life. This situation is not uncommon these days.

In contrast, self-worth, confidence, forgiveness and money are the root of most of the affirmations I teach due to the commonality of students I work with. Only upon working together one on one did LJ and I dive deep into his background so I could learn his early environment, see his blocks and help him address them. These were uncomfortable conversations, but he handled the pushback and pressure from me well.

We focused his affirmation work on confidence and self-worth. Slowly but surely, writing daily, he saw the true power and potential he had within himself and began to tell himself he was worthy and speak it into existence, embodying the reality of rewriting his belief system daily through affirmations.

He evolved as a human and within a year, LJ went from low confidence and lost with low self-worth to being happy, always smiling and believing in himself. He grew into a man of pride of himself, his family and business. And, of course, he also made much more money. This will only continue as he walks the rocky road journey of letting go of false realities as he now understands we are the only ones who can create our lives, our futures and realities.

The thoughts we write daily with a pen and paper force our minds to accept the truth through autosuggestion, making thoughts develop into existence. This is called "manifesting what you desire of into reality."

TYPES OF AFFIRMATIONS

Affirmations must be written in a positive light; always be positive while writing and speaking affirmations and articulate them in the present tense to write and speak them into existence. There are endless affirmations—thousands, if not tens of thousands to pick from to write, listen to and adapt as yours. The key to selecting affirmations is to find pre-written affirmations or build your own that LIGHT YOU UP.

We'd never want to just go through the motions while writing affirmations. Think about it—what would that do? Not too much...and down the line, you'd be asking yourself, "Why aren't I breaking my patterns and manifesting all I desire?" We write and speak affirmations into existence by emotionally lighting up while executing them.

Let's look at this from the lens of sex. We're associating these because no one likes boring, mundane, meaningless, going-through-the-motion sex. We've all been there, maybe early on when first starting out with sex or maybe right now in your relationship, but somewhere along the way, we've all had sex that just didn't do it for us due to many reasons...or just one.

Say you were with a partner and the sex was dull. You went through the motions for years, but really wanted to have better sex. You'd come to a point when you'd start asking yourself why the sex isn't better. Then you'd try to fix the problem, whether through counseling, reading books, YouTube videos or maybe even a new partner. With practice, you'd find yourself and your partner had better, more enjoyable sex.

Now focus on affirmations. The last thing you'll want to do is pick affirmations that aren't fun, that don't light you up, that you don't feel within you while writing them. Know the difference between an affirmation that doesn't light you up and affirmations you love.

However, even a carefully chosen affirmation might occasionally feel tiresome as you write it daily. There will be times when the affirmation you love feels off or low vibe. Recognize that it's you who's off or lower vibe than usual. With practice, you'll grasp the difference just like anything else. Practice makes perfect.

Now, back to the types of affirmations because you understand how important it is to pick the proper affirmations to manifest all you desire. The two types of affirmations we focus on in this book are the affirmations that changed my life and thousands if not tens of thousands of others: forgiveness- and money-centric affirmations.

As we explore both forgiveness and money affirmations, Catherine Ponder, in my humble opinion, is the queen of both, to include affirmations as a whole. You might disagree, but the sheer amount of content she's produced during her long career can't be denied. She has the most affirmations I've seen and hers are the affirmations that helped change not only mine, but most of my students' lives over the years.

Most people haven't a clue just how deeply they've buried feelings other than positive for those in their life from the present back to childhood. Ironically, the more work you put into forgiving, the more situations and people come to light who need your forgiveness. Your forgiveness not only frees them, but more importantly, frees yourself from the negativity you unknowingly harbor inside yourself.

FORGIVENESS

I can't overstress the importance of forgiveness affirmations. Many people, including myself, fail to realize how much negativity we hold on to as we move through our lives. Even though we may not think we're holding on to negativity, the chances are we are. There can be negativity surrounding events, experiences and people we deal with day to day in different stages of our lives.

In this book, I'll often discuss how pivotal our early environments are—your environment has shaped you into the person you are today. And if you were raised anything like I was, you were taught to just deal with the pain, whether physical or emotional.

As a boy growing up in the '80s and '90s, my father raised me to be tough; he was a manly man. If something hurtful happened to me, he would have taught me to deal with it and then suppress my feelings. Whether he knew it or not—and I'm guessing not—he was teaching me to hide and bury my negative and angry feelings toward subjects and people.

Growing through life and through my studies of human psychology, I realized what I was taught in my early environment isn't healthy. As I played sports, I was taught the same.

Of course, once landing in the military, all of that unhealthy upbringing was reinforced and built upon.

Most interestingly, our bodies and minds don't know the difference between positive and negative thoughts. When we say negative things, feel negative responses and speak negatively, our bodies bury the negativity within us. If you were raised similar to me, you might now realize you have years, if not decades, of negativity buried within you. Sadly, our mainstream media, social media, movies, newspapers and magazines alike are the biggest culprits of at times being unknowingly negative and providing an environment that furthers widely accepted normality of negativity.

I want you to take the time to think about people in your past and present and then focus on anyone with whom you had a falling out or a serious disagreement. Try to recall if you said anything negative to or about them. Take the same time considering traumatic events you've experienced in life. Think hard about anything you may have spoken negatively about, as this will be the focus of the forgiveness affirmations you'll be learning to write.

This will be the fuel to work on and will undo years of negativity you've had and have now decided to change by working on yourself. Most humans won't put the time or effort into this type of inner work. That's precisely why your life will change and theirs might not, and never will. If you'd like to hear more, open YouTube and search for "Chris Warnes Forgiveness."

As you focus on forgiveness affirmations, for a time—and the amount of time will differ from person to person—things might be bumpy until you get used to it. This is called "kicking the beehive." The bees will come out to sting you, metaphorically speaking. However, the short-term pain you'll experience from kicking this beehive is well worth the long-term freedom that will follow.

Another way of looking at this bumpiness of the road you're traveling is the beginning of a "leveling up," even to a small degree. When we start to work on undoing years of negativity, along with possibly judgment, hatred and cynicism, we're releasing anything that no longer serves us, our thoughts of that subject, event or person.

This will create two things: First, as you kick the beehive, you'll stir up feelings and thoughts about people and events you didn't know you had until partaking on this journey.

Some common signs you might notice of the beehive being kicked are sleepless nights, your mind racing on about events or people you hadn't thought about in years, and even your skin breaking out due to your body releasing toxins. The metaphysical response from a body is profound.

My beehive kick is ongoing the more I release and forgive. The first sign I was releasing and forgiving was that chronic pain I had from the war was disappearing left and right. First was my knees: Pain in both sides was just vanishing. Then, my memory was coming back through all sorts of long- and short-term memories. I felt like a new man with this.

For over a decade, I played victim to being wounded in Iraq, blaming my lack of memory on the powerful bomb that struck me. However, I later realized I was wrong. Then, my lower back pain vanished. Pain I'd dealt with for more than 10 years was basically gone overnight.

As I write this, the last piece of the pie, metaphysically speaking from forgiving and releasing, is the full ability to hear. I've had tinnitus and hearing loss since the war; some of my hearing has returned, but it's not entirely back, which is my way of knowing I have more work to do. Many of my students have experienced the same result of chronic pain leaving their bodies, including veterans who suffered from the same issues I once did. You, too, might cure your pain by taking control of your life and forgiving all in your past and present.

Room for good to enter your life is the second thing you'll create in your life by focusing on forgiveness affirmations. Think about it this way: If we suppress and bury our thoughts and feelings for years, once we address our behavior by learning to and then releasing the negativity by a forgiveness affirmations practice, we'll create room for more to enter our lives.

In terms of this material, we'll make room for good to enter our lives as we now have the space to store only positive thoughts. This is where the real life-changing happens because not only will you see more good come into your life, but you'll also hear from people in your life you've forgiven as they randomly reach out to you to apologize or to pick back up where you left off. If this happens, go with it, allow it and hear their level of forgiveness back to you.

However, something profound will happen, and it takes time. Now that you're aware of how you were speaking or thinking negatively into your life, you'll start to reframe your thoughts and words. You'll know why you're doing this forgiveness work and will naturally want to limit the amount of work you create for yourself. You'll begin to not only notice, but also change the words and thoughts a more optimistic tone.

For instance, if I had a negative thought about a person or situation after learning this, I'd catch the thought in the moment, repeat it back to be sure what I thought or said was actually negative, and then reframe it, thinking only of the subject in a positive light.

An example of catching and reframing would be when you're upset about something that has just happened and you say something hateful or pessimistic about an event or person. You notice what you said, think about what you said and say it differently under a positive lens of focus. This is called "reframing" and is a lifesaver.

Here's an example of a reframe:

Negative: Wow, the president has no clue what the heck he's talking about when it comes to this topic.

When you catch yourself talking negatively, simply go back and reword the sentence.

Positive: With more research and understanding of the topic, our president could deliver a moving speech.

The key is to catch it and when you see it, be ready.

There will be more than you might know what to do with—

the work will be plentiful reframing your thoughts and words.

HOW-TO: AN EXAMPLE OF FORGIVENESS AFFIRMATIONS

Focusing on forgiveness affirmations on people you feel the want or need to forgive is a great place to start and continue exploring. However, commonly, the number one person who requires forgiveness—and in turn, who forgiveness should be centered around—is you.

You're the most powerful person to center your forgiveness around. If you start with yourself, you won't regret it as it opens the doors to forgive others in your life.

Forgiving yourself for things you did and the decisions made is the most powerful thing you can do for yourself in this work. You may not even realize that you need forgiveness, but as you embark on this journey, you'll change.

Now let's take a look at some examples of forgiveness affirmations. These are some of the most powerful and favorite I've come across; however, I encourage you to explore more and build your own. I'll use myself as the example for the sake of the exercise.

1. Christopher—I let loose and let go. All ill feelings are cleared up now and forever. I rejoice that no good thing can be withheld from the forgiving state of mind.

2. I love everyone and everyone loves me; I love myself and am loved. I forgive everyone and everyone forgives me; I forgive myself and am forgiven. I bless everyone and everyone blesses me; I bless myself and am blessed.

3. Christopher—All that has offended me, I forgive. Within and without, I forgive. Things past, things present, things future, I forgive. I forgive everything and everybody who needs forgiveness in the past or present. I positively forgive everyone. I'm free and they're free too. All things are cleared up between us now and forever.

4. I now let go worn-out things, worn-out conditions,

worn-out relationships. Divine order is now established and maintained in me and in my world.

5. I know the release is magnetic. Through the act of release, I draw to myself my own. I now fully and freely release. I let loose and let go. I let go and grow. I let go and trust.

6. I bless the past and forget it. I bless the future, knowing it's filled with wonderful opportunities and successes. I live fully in the present now and am blessed with all I desire or require. Any mistakes of my past are now transformed into my good.

7. When I look at this situation in the rearview mirror of life, I'll see how the universe turned this situation into my good.

8. I bless, love and forgive everyone, and everyone blesses, loves and forgives me. I bless, love and forgive myself.

9. There are no mistakes in the all-knowing power. Therefore, there are no mistakes in my life.

10. _____ (insert name), I bless you, I love you, I forgive you, I release you.

Now that you have a small selection of forgiveness affirmations to choose from, use them all, begin with and then focus on the one or two that REALLY LIGHT YOU UP.

You'll feel it. You'll know which lands better than the rest... the one or two that resonate with you.

Later in the chapter, I'll speak more on writing, when to write and how often to write these affirmations. Along with our next set of affirmations, we'll discuss money affirmations, the key to prosperity with a spiritual approach.

LESSONS LEARNED FROM FORGIVENESS AFFIRMATIONS

I had a conversation with my mother about the power of forgiveness and the affirmations centered on forgiveness she could use around some family members to help with some pent-up long-term anger. Before we go into detail, I encourage you to look at your family relationships, including siblings and parents, because many people don't realize how much forgiveness is needed in these human relationships.

My mother and I were speaking about how to forgive her brother for decades of mistreatment or perceived mistreatment and less-than-ideal situations. I assigned her reading material and what to do affirmation-wise, and she went to work. Within a month, she called to tell me about a phone call from her brother after several years of not speaking and the call going well overall.

This is an example of clearing out the negativity around someone or something and allowing good to come into your life, or, as in this case, forgiveness on both ends of a relationship. The first step is forgiving people in your life, then you'll experience events, just as my mother did.

MONEY AFFIRMATIONS

Now that we understand we need to forgive ourselves and others, creating room for good to come into our lives, we can conceptualize the more we work on forgiveness, the more space we create for money to come into our lives. The longer we work on forgiving, the more money will come into your life because there's a direct relationship.

It wasn't until I embodied this practice that I passed what I thought at that time to be a daunting seven-figure mark. The more time I put into forgiving, the more room I created for money to come my way.

One of the most challenging years I experienced in business, 2020, with the onset of a global recession masked by a worldwide pandemic of COVID 19 is a great example of how well both forgiveness and money affirmations go hand and hand to create money when it was most needed. After years of doing both affirmations, I got to a place where everywhere I went, money was chasing me.

For example, almost every time I get out of the car at a gas station, I look down and there's money on the ground, from pennies to large bills. Before we explain areas in life that can be opportunities to discover random money, let me pass along a lesson my grandfather gave me when I was a young boy.

Some context is needed about my grandfather. Joseph Letterio grew up a poor Italian immigrant, one of 11 siblings, in New Haven CT.

When Joe was 11 years old, his father died, forcing all siblings, including Joe, to drop out of school and to help support the family so they could survive.

My grandfather got a job pushing a broom at an old warehouse specializing in commercial flatware for restaurants. Some years later, the owners of the warehouse sold the company to my grandfather. He then built it into a multimillion-dollar company. He was a man of few words and was quietly very wealthy.

Back to the lesson: When I was a boy, he took me to lunch. On our way back to his car, he stopped and bent down, picked up a rusty penny and put it into his pocket.

I don't recall the exact words I said to him. However, the gist was, "Grandpa, why are you picking up pennies? You're rich." That's when he turned my world upside down and unknowingly gave me my first entrepreneurial lesson in finance, saying as he bent down to look me in the face, "Christopher, it's one penny more than I had waking up today."

Going back to the gas station example now as a grown man, I always find and pick up change. After decades of doing this, I've found thousands of dollars a year from this habit. If we put it into perspective, a couple thousand dollars a year saved is not only enough for a down payment on a new car, but after a few years, it's enough money to put down on your first home.

"It's one penny more than I had when I woke up this morning."
**~ Joseph Letterio, a poor immigrant
turned self-made multi-millionaire**

Before the first quarter of 2020, all my businesses were doing well and growing financially. However, once the pandemic hit, I saw money affirmations working on a grand scale.

Government grants put in place for struggling businesses due to the pandemic would be deposited into my accounts with little work to capture them, collecting almost $90,000 from the government and another $40,000 of manifested money with no sales or service attached to the funds, totaling $130,000 of extra unearned for cash finding its way to me, rather than me chasing money by working for it.

Money affirmations do an excellent job of rewriting our belief system about money. Many of us grew up middle class or poor, and being raised like this, we learn how our parents or whoever raised us think about and value money. Believing that money is "wrong" is a perfect example of a "poor" money mindset.

Money is great, especially when we look at it for what it is, a tool and leverage. Money allows us more—more of anything, to include the ability to build anything we desire. In business, the more money you can generate, the more people you can employ, the more you can affect your community, the more you can donate, the better the quality of your life, the more you can help humans, potentially changing humanity if that's your focus, with examples like Elon Musk and Jeff Bezos.

How we look at money can be the root of all evil. When we look at money as a never-ending source of supply, as leverage to achieve more, that we deserve to have all the money we desire to help with our mission, passion and purpose on this earth, we have a wealthy and healthy money mindset opposed to how many of us were raised, with a poor money mindset.

What many of us were taught about saving money is another commonly overlooked and misunderstood example of a poor money mindset. Save your money for a rainy day—does that sound familiar?

There are degrees of truth; however, keeping all your money, not putting it to work as the tool it is, more or plentiful amounts won't come. This is precisely what we're talking about when considering a poor money mindset.

When we look at money as it's constantly flowing to us—however much of it we want and that the universe supplies us with the money we need—we learn what a wealthy money mindset looks like. We become a money magnet and understand there's gold dust in the air for us all.

Next, let's discuss how to apply affirmations. Now that you understand how powerful money affirmations are, rewriting your belief system on money, shifting you from poor money mindset to wealthy, moving you out of a scarcity mindset, and redirecting you to a money magnet mindset where all you desire WILL BE.

I'll provide you with some money affirmations to get started. The key is to write them all and then find the affirmations that land with you the best, lighting you up, FEELING THEM as you write and think about them.

1. I don't depend on people or conditions for my prosperity. I bless people and conditions as channels of my prosperity, the universe (insert the word God, source, passed relative, assistors—whatever you believe to be your source) is the source of my supply. The universe provides its own amazing channels of supply now.

2. I'm the rich child of a loving Father so I prosper now.

3. I dissolve in my own mind, and in the minds of all others, any idea that my prosperity can be withheld from me. No person, thing or event can keep from me that which the universe has for me now.

4. My financial income cannot be limited. The rich substance of the universe frees me from financial limitations. I know that release is magnetic. Through the act of release, I draw to myself my own. I now fully and freely release.

5. I let loose and let go. I let go and grow. I let go and trust.

6. I let go of worn-out things, worn-out conditions, worn-out relationships. Divine order is now established and

maintained in me and in my world.

7. Vast improvement comes quickly in every phase of my life. Every day in every way, things are getting better and better for me now.

8. I invite the wealth of the universe to richly manifest in my financial affairs. I'm rich in mind and manifestation.

9. I have a large, steady, dependable and permanent financial income. Every day in every way, I'm growing more and more financially prosperous now.

10. Large sums of money, big happy financial surprises and rich gifts now come under grace in perfect ways for my personal use, and I use them wisely.

11. I give thanks for a quick and substantial increase in my financial income.

12. I'm rich, well and happy, and every phase of my life is in divine order now.

13. I praise my world.

14. I praise my financial affairs. All the wealth that hasn't come in the past is manifesting richly for me now.

15. The enormous sums of money that are mine by divine right now manifest for me quickly and in peace.

16. I give thanks for the immediate and complete payment of all financial obligations, quickly and in peace.

17. I'm receiving. I'm receiving now. I'm receiving all the wealth the universe has for me.

18. All that the rich substance of the universe has for me comes speedily, richly and freely. My rich good now comes quickly and in peace.

BUSINESS-CENTRIC MONEY AFFIRMATIONS

1. Spirit (insert who you pray to) now guides and directs me in all my affairs. My business is experiencing increased sales and profits.

2. My business is taking off with a huge increase in sales. All related to this are blessed by it.

3. Spirit guides me to never-ending supply, and I accept and receive the huge success that's mine.

APPLICATION OF AFFIRMATIONS

The consistent application of favorite affirmations, the affirmations that LIGHT US UP while writing them and speaking them into existence has worked best for students I've worked with, along with myself, to embody the practice of affirmations.

I recommend writing your favorite affirmation at least 10 times daily. Yes, write the same affirmation you feel within you 10 times in a row, ideally in one sitting. This is the minimum I recommend, and in the grand scheme of things, will be better than not doing at all.

Writing three sets of 10 affirmations daily until you look at money and the feeling of money differently will work wonders, as it did for me and many students who needed serious rewriting of their subconscious, specifically their scarcity mindset.

How long it will take for a mindset to shift is different for everyone. This process takes time—weeks, months and even years. If you find you have a serious scarcity mindset around money or what I described earlier in this chapter as a "poor money mindset," writing your affirmation three times a day will greatly help put you in the proper direction quicker. Catherine Ponder says that writing an affirmation 15 times in a row has produced magical results for her students in the past. I support this application 15 times in a row too. I tried it, and it yielded a faster mindset growth.

There's no right or wrong way to do this. If you write your daily affirmations on money and forgiveness, you'll change your mindset. If you write your favorite affirmations during your morning routine, it will work. If you write your favorite affirmations three times a day in sets of 10 or 15, it will work...likely faster. However, if you find yourself thinking of scarcity around money, take out your journal and start writing at that moment. This will help you change your mindset faster.

For example, say you have rent due at the beginning of the month and you find yourself stressing over the payment. Take out your journal and start writing your affirmations at that moment, replacing scarcity thoughts with abundance thoughts.

Do this every time scarcity creeps into your mind. Before you know it, you'll have rewritten the way your mind thinks about money, knowing there's gold dust in the air. You're a money magnet; the universe, as a source, will always give you what you desire and are a vibrational match for.

Ask and you shall receive. Give and you'll get. The first step is to be willing to give and graciously receive. Money vibes all day long are the vibes that create more.

It's now your time to be a vibrational match for all you desire. GO WRITE SOME AFFIRMATIONS and start on the path of living the life you dream of.

> *"Open up your minds, find that spark inside*
> *Time to focus, realize, good things take their time*
> *And suddenly a glitter of a light shines bright*
> *Possessing me with all of which I need to speak my mind*
> *Ask me, will I stop, no way*
> *'Cause your energy just dropped, no not today*
> *Ask me, will I stop*
> *We keep it rocking all day, let it all soak in*
> *I've been working, I've been working all night long*
> *Trying to find the spark, finding out what I'm doing wrong*
> *No problem I got time to focus on*
> *I got some passion and more patience than I thought."*
> **~ Stick Figure featuring Eric Rachmany**
> *(From Mind Block, used with permission)*

PRO TIP: SPEAK THINGS INTO EXISTENCE

A key that works wonders is very similar to spoken prayer. Once you've written out your affirmations, whether they be forgiveness, money or any other affirmations you want to write, get into the habit of reading them out loud after writing them. For example, say you've written 10 forgiveness affirmations and 10 money affirmations during your morning routine session.

Now, go to a quiet place if you're not already there or, better yet, stand in front of a mirror and read out loud the affirmations you've just written. Read them with emotion; speak them into existence with POWERFUL words, meaning the words as you're reading them.

As you become better at speaking your affirmations into existence, you'll notice a significant change in your life at the moment of speaking. When you speak with emotion, loudly and meaningfully, you'll feel a tingling sensation within your body. You've felt it before, maybe listening to your favorite song or talking about a deceased relative. You know the feeling and the more you feel this, the more you'll speak into existence and the quicker it will come.

This is when you're becoming a vibrational match for whatever you desire, whatever you're writing about, whatever your affirmations and whatever you're speaking into existence.

I also recommend reading your gratitude journal aloud after completion. SPEAK IT ALL INTO EXISTENCE. Everything you want, all that you desire—don't hold back, have it all. It's your birthright to be wealthy.

Before we move into the next chapter and the lesson of leisure time, let's touch on something that may happen on your journey of affirmations, writing daily about all that you desire, all that you want, changing your mindset and rewriting your subconscious. Something very natural might happen that we've all experienced after journeying down this road: the feeling of going through the motions.

A point may come when you just aren't feeling it, when you aren't vibing…nothing is manifesting. You're just stale because you've been putting so much time and effort into your affirmations. It's normal, and that's key to understanding when or if you experience this. It's natural. It happens to all of us, especially if you're writing seven days a week, as many of us do. It's okay to take a break from writing.

This may happen with your daily gratitude journaling too, and that's the time to take a break from the writing. We want the writing of affirmations and gratitude journaling to be fun, to feel it when you write it, to vibe with it, to smile and enjoy it.

Suppose this point comes when you're not feeling it. You don't want to go through the motions or fall into that pattern. If that's the case, not only is it not fun, you might not be manifesting and rewriting your subconscious as quickly as you can. Just step back and take a break for a few days or more. If you need a week, it's okay to take it, then jump back into it.

The key is to vibe with the process and HAVE FUN.

GOLD DUST IS IN THE AIR

I want to share with you some big wins students of this course have received. A friend who took the *Dominate Your Day* course was in a job he wasn't fond of and told me he wanted a significant change in his life. With the principles taught here, including money affirmations, within about eight weeks, he manifested $10,000, quit his job and opened a gym. Within a year of opening his gym, he has now partnered and bought a second business.

Another friend who came to learn how to build a life of success manifested $6,000 within a few weeks of learning money affirmations I teach in the course. He invested that money back into himself, knowing he will always be his best investment.

A member of my team who learned these principles manifested $2,800 out of thin air deposited into her bank account. To this day, there's no explanation why, other than she believed there was gold dust in the air.

A single mother and disabled veteran put these principles to work and almost immediately manifested just over $120,000, which she put into her business. We celebrated her win together, and she is on a roll of manifesting everywhere.

Several of my students manifested job promotions, to the tune of $40,000 extra a year with the raise. Manifesting money and large sums of it is just a matter of being a vibrational match for all you desire. You can experience this too. It all starts with your daily money affirmations.

CHAPTER 5

LEISURE TIME

I remember exactly where I was when I first discovered the value of leisure time. The weight of it hit me like getting hit in the face by a Mac truck and then crashing through a brick wall. The subject hit me so hard, I knew I had to make a change in my life. If I didn't implement leisure time ASAP, I'd continue to not only burn the candle at both ends, but lose more of what I didn't want to lose in life by being married to a job I wasn't enjoying and wasn't fulfilling or purposeful.

It was late 2018, around Christmas. My life was at a fascinating point, one I'd never been to before. I was successful, had a couple of companies, big staff, nice cars, vacationing around the country, was asked to speak at events, was looked up to, interviewed often, befriended by many and made great money. I thought I was doing well.

However, if you looked below the surface, it was a much different story. To the untrained eye, I owned a company that was doing well, but on the inside, everything was a mess. The managers I had in place shouldn't have been managing, which was my fault. Work quality was poor, which customers occasionally saw; most things were accomplished last minute and to top it all off, if I didn't do the task, the chances of it being done with quality were low—everything from payroll to marketing, customer service, to sales, booking appointments to mentoring and coaching.

I wasn't happy with the work or myself. This was all my responsibility. As an owner of a company, the faster you realize all your company's shortcomings are ultimately yours, the faster you'll rectify the situation.

On top of the mess at the company, I also left a relationship I should have left years before, only in hindsight realizing it was toxic and abusive. I didn't speak to my closest friends very often, never saw my family and when I did, I was rushed getting there and while there, I was agitated and quick to leave.

There I was one morning in Vermont before a day of snowboarding, reading a book from one of my favorite authors, Dale Carnegie: *The Leader in You*. It had taken me a lot of planning to make that snowboarding trip happen and when I arrived, I felt like a ton of bricks had been lifted off my chest, leaving the daily grind behind. Leisure time wasn't valued then. It was looked down upon as the Instagram hustle mentality of grind grind grind 24 hours a day, seven days a week was the only acceptable lifestyle at that point…because, why not?

For nearly a decade prior, grinding around the clock had gotten me where I was in life. However, I didn't know how much I was missing inside my soul from not taking time for myself all those years. I'd learned, in that very moment, that I was wrong in my outlook on work, let alone life. There had to have been an important reason the words from Carnegie resonated with me so deeply when he wrote that all high performers who live beautiful lives with their families and friends take a lot of time for themselves.

I knew at that very moment things would change; I knew I had work to do on myself. I knew I had to schedule my leisure time, lay boundaries down for myself and hold myself accountable to having some fun, and often.

These are some of the words that stood out that day:

"There is nothing wrong with material success, but that alone is not enough to sustain a happy life.

"How can you start balancing your life? The first step is to change your attitude. You've got to stop thinking of your time for your family, for exercise, or for leisure as wasted time.

"Achievers often feel they need to apologize for leisure time. Try to rid yourself of that thought. Relaxation is not a dirty word. You have to make time for leisure activity. Most of us are over-committed.

"Perhaps it's time to reevaluate priorities. Decide to devote as much energy to planning your leisure time as you devote to planning your workday."

~ Dale Carnegie

As I finished reading those words, I dropped the book with the bookmark in place, picked up my gear, headed to the mountain and had a fantastic day with friends, not for one moment feeling guilty about missing work or work calls. From that very point on, I took my leisure time seriously, building leisure into my schedule and enjoying many things I'd forgotten I loved.

Consider how you can go about not only remembering things you love, but how to schedule them into your day to day, so your leisure time gas tank is always full.

The first step is to take some time to figure out what you love to do that isn't work-related. You might love your work, as I do. However, we need to focus on non-work-related activities to fill up that leisure gas tank.

Using myself as the example, shortly after that landmark day, I took to my notebook, brainstormed and wrote down several things I love to do ranging from playing poker with friends, going out to eat because I love great food, wine and excellent conversation, shooting guns, shooting pool, hiking, snowboarding, walking my dogs, working out in the gym and just lying on the couch reflecting on my day.

The key here is to search your soul deeply and find what LIGHTS YOU UP. Nothing is off-limits other than work. Think deep, meditate on it if you need to and come up with your list of passions and fun leisure activities you want to do. These can be anything from spending time with your family, walking the dog, swimming, watching movies, reading, writing, anything… the longer the list, the better. After you spend some time coming up with these leisure time activities, you'll be ready to learn how to schedule these.

I will explain precisely what I do and teach my students to ensure time to spend on what LIGHTS UP YOUR SOUL.

FAMILY TIME

Many of us have blood-related family and some don't. "Family" need not be contained to where you came from as a human. Family can be many situations, from soldiers you serve with, friends who have gotten so close you can call them brother, sister, mom, dad, aunt or uncle. Family represents those closest to you, regardless of sharing the same blood coursing through your veins.

Spending time with your family, whether it's your significant relationship, with children or those you've grown so close to they feel like family should be at the top of your list of leisure time to reap the full benefits of leisure time, of refilling your energy, and also life. Those family parties you're invited to, like birthday parties, graduation parties, holiday gatherings and anytime of celebration are something you should be a part of no matter how many companies you own and how much you need to do at work. Besides, if you're working long, hard hours, your staff will be happy that you leave early or don't come in, not only for your sake but also for theirs.

Family leisure time does not have to be limited to parties and gatherings. I had a student tell me how he wanted to change his life, but couldn't get out of the cycle of partying and drinking with his friends often, including every weekend. In the same breath, he'd tell me how much his grandmother meant to him and that he never saw her.

After some time, we got him to see the situation by stepping aside from his feelings and outwardly observing his actions. We shifted his time and energy by primarily spending it with his family and grandmother, going for daily walks and hanging out with one another while putting aside the toxicity of partying.

This is a perfect example of allocating energy properly to those who need and deserve your time and energy by reallocating your leisure time to be beneficial to you and your family.

No matter what, through thick and thin, your family, whether blood related or not, will be who are there for you when you need them most, when you hit rock bottom and need a helping hand up. Spend your time with them, visit them, go for walks, travel with them, be with them and prioritize your leisure time for, as they say in my culture, *la familia*.

DATE NIGHT

If you're in any relationship, whether or not it's traditional, it's vitally important to keep a healthy, thriving relationship alive by never stopping the fundamentals the relationship was founded upon. When two people are getting to know each other, they're excited to see one another and typically to go out on dates. Dating, or courting one another, is standard practice at the start of any relationship, but slips away as time goes on.

There's a typical pattern of complacency in longer-term relationships. We've all been there; we get used to our partners and stop courting them in the manner we did at the beginning when getting to know one another.

Since we're looking through the lens of leisure time, date night is a perfect addition to your leisure time plans that will keep your relationship happy, healthy and romantic, basically killing two birds with one stone. I recommend weekly date nights if you're in the financial place to do so. However, even monthly is better than none.

Date night doesn't have to be a fancy dinner and if fancy dinners aren't in the cards for you, remember that getting dressed up and going to Target or simply food shopping is just as good when you're on a budget. Something is better than nothing. "Trying" in a relationship goes a long way. Being consistent with dates, courting and self-improvement will be significant for you and your partner. For more ideas, open YouTube and search for "Chris Warnes Relationship Goals."

Suppose you're in a place to go out to dinner weekly. I want to speak to the gentlemen reading this. Ladies, if reading this leaves you speechless, buy a copy of this book and give it as a gift to the man in your life. I'll fill you in on why the man in your life may not be doing some of these ideas later in the chapter.

The masculine energy is a powerful one that's no stronger or more powerful than feminine energy. They're ying and yang to one another, balancing each other. However, men, as the masculine energy in the relationship, it's your job to set up the date. Gentlemen, trust me, your wife, girlfriend or side chick wants you to take the lead not only on setting up dates, but in the entire relationship.

Let's say weekly date night is Friday night. You're not going to walk up to your partner like a beaten puppy and ask, "Honey, where do you want to go for date night?" Your partner desperately wants you to pick the restaurant or venue, and also call ahead or book reservations online for a specific time. Tell her she's the most beautiful person you've ever seen, put her jacket on her if the weather calls for it, hold the door for her, pull her chair out, order the drinks, appetizers and main course for you and her.

If you do all this, the chances of her being blown away will be a 9.9 out of 10, especially if you're the guy who usually acts like a whipped puppy dog. You'll set her curiosity on fire. You'll stir up her feminine energy. She'll be blown away by your confidence and decision-making ability. This is what she's always wanted. Treat her with respect, treat her like a delicate flower, act like you're the man and you, my friend, will get very lucky not just at the end of the date, but more often than normal.

Ladies, what you just read isn't a mythical man who's extinct. There are men who embody masculine energy and the practice of stepping up to the plate. We're a rarity, few and far between. We're proud, we're confident, masculine and, most importantly, we're centered. If you're with a man and want to see him act like that, you'll need to step back and let him step into his role. The chances are, you don't let him; you may be in your masculine energy without even realizing it, which is common.

The best way to see this happen isn't just telling him what you want. It will take more work to get him to step up.

Encourage it and give him positive reinforcement. Take the time to tell him what you'd love to see him do, like calling ahead, setting a reservation and holding the door. Tell him that when he does things like that, you're turned on by him being such a manly man (or whatever is suitable).

When you tell a man something turns you on, you'll have his full attention; he's listening, especially if you aren't having the most sex because you've both become complacent in the relationship. Ladies, when you step back into your feminine energy, this is always a signal to the man you're with to step forward into his masculine energy. It's okay to step aside and let him take the ropes; he probably wants the ropes and wants to make you happy, and also to impress you with his ability to be a man.

If you continue to tell him this, things will shift. When you say that something's hot or it turns you on, be sure to follow through with playful and fun sex at the end of the night because if you don't, he'll catch on that you're bluffing and will quickly step back into his disempowered masculine energy...or even possibly his feminine energy.

Back to date night: Never forget how important it is to continue courting your partner. You want to consistently remind her, even gently, that you're wild for her and love her.

I was working with a student who'd been married for some time, somewhere along the lines of 10 years. When we started working together, we focused on other things in his life, such as his self-development and career.

One day we got around to shooting the shit about his family when we were dealing with a situation of him losing control in front of his family. I then found out that what was happening was the reality of most couples who have been together for years. They tend to take each other for granted due to time spent together and the growing complacency.

We started to unpack the dynamic between he and his wife and found he'd slipped into his disempowered masculine, which is typical for guys who have the thought process of "happy wife, happy life" as they bend over backward, often sacrificing peace of mind to keep her happy. Sadly, men often slip into this energy and don't even know it.

I then discovered he and his wife were in this poor energy dynamic, not going out, dating or sleeping together. We addressed that after I pointed out what had been happening, focusing on how to improve things, which was simple because he loved and adored his wife and family. The change was quick and straightforward; he did precisely as written earlier, with the only addition of him dressing up in a collared shirt, which he otherwise didn't do often.

Within 12 weeks, the shift was rapid and the relationship was better. I remember where I was when I read the message that his wife was pregnant with their second child soon after this reallocation of energy dynamic in their relationship.

Have fun with your relationship—court, date and be in the traditional energies to ensure your coveted leisure time will go well. Date night and leisure time go hand and hand and I only hope you're stepping in the right direction to ensure both quality and priority in your life.

A man or woman who is truly successful has the family and leisure time prioritized and lives harmoniously with the family's relationships. A well-balanced, successful life is one that all should live as it's the most rewarding experience we humans can be a part of.

YOUR FRIENDS

Let's quickly touch upon how the leisure time spent with friends is as important as that with family and mates. We can be quick to think that getting together with our closest friends can be a waste of time as there's more work that we can be done. But the exciting part is how much better our job is when our energy and our soul is full. That's the point; it's simple to make an ego-based justification that we can get so much work done during the few hours we'd normally spend with friends.

But the truth behind the matter is, the more time you cut out for yourself without sacrificing important work and deadlines, the better the quality of your work will always be. When you're invited out, there's an event or your friend wants to come over or call you on the phone and catch up, remember you're filling your cup up with good times, good vibes and good energy. All of this together will help you be the best version of yourself, which will produce the best work product.

This monumental and potentially life-changing chapter is here to teach you to take care of yourself and your well-being because the people in your life are the people who will be there for you when you need them most.

Take care of yourself, take care of them and you'll have nothing to worry about as all will fall into place in doing so. The universe sees you, hears you and will put all you ask for in front of you. Be lush with your leisure time, as your leisure time will be lush with you for years to come.

Now that we have that out of the way, it's time to move into our next chapter, a chapter written on a movement I don't take credit for. However, I've decided to live by it and teach it to any-one who will listen, attempting to change humanity one human at a time on the topic of BEING A GOOD HUMAN.

CHAPTER 6

BE A GOOD HUMAN

Human nature is inherently selfish. Most people have no clue their nature and behavior are selfish. The depth of selfishness is buried deep inside our bodies and minds. Human narcissistic tendencies are neither here nor there, but are important to understand as we're focused on adopting a new mindset.

Being a good human is selfless, embodying selflessness to its fullest degree. Being a good human isn't to post your act of kindness on the 'Gram, but for 100 percent of the time you're awake. It's not for "likes" on social media, but for a better humanity by being selfless; it's not to impress your friends, but to help someone in need. It's not to brag about to your family, but to help change someone's life. Being a good human starts from the moment you open your eyes in the morning and should last until you shut them at night—daily, for the rest of your life. Go to YouTube and search for "Chris Warnes Be a Good Human" for more details.

Being a good human comes into play with everything you do daily. Many call karma the ultimate observer, to serve you what you deserve, and I agree. However, there's a principle that holds a lot of value and weight among the right audience: *willingly give and graciously receive.* It means you'll receive back 10 or 100-fold whatever you provide. What we put out into the world is what comes back.

This isn't a new topic. It's been around for thousands of years, first discussed in the Bible as *"For whatever a man sows, this he will also reap."* There are countless ways to look at being a good human and the principle that comes with it; the most significant takeaway is that the universe is always watching you and your actions. Your actions are magnetic; you put good out into the world and you'll attract only what you deserve, only more good to come.

And on the contrary, if you put less than good, anything wrong, deceitful, cynical or negative, it will come back to you. Know this concept and put your good out to receive bountiful amounts of great.

Since we've discussed the big picture of how the universe sees you and that your actions are magnetic, let's step back and focus on the day-to-day activities you can do to embody being a good human. I've listed examples of some low-hanging fruit.

THE SHOPPING CART

The "shopping cart" is one of my favorite examples of how easy it is to be an excellent human and how selfish many are, most of the time without even knowing so. This example puts on display how knowingly doing the wrong thing is more common than some realize: The majority of Americans don't put their shopping cart away once they get their groceries to their car.

If you're reading this and saying to yourself, "Damn, I guess this is me Chris is talking about," even though I'm talking about you, I'm also talking about myself—I didn't return my carts to the proper place in my younger days. It's okay if you haven't been putting your shopping carts away because from this point on, you're going to take the extra 30 to 60 seconds it takes to put your cart away as you embody being a good human.

I don't recall precisely when I started putting my carts away when I was finished with them; I do remember the looks on other faces as I'd watch them finish with their carts, leave them next to their cars or maybe give a little effort and prop their cart up on the curb or sidewalk once they were done with them. Then I'd come along, smiling ear to ear, grab the cart, look them in the eye and push it back to the cart corral for them. Typically, a mouth would drop wide open or they'd speed off out of the parking lot, likely embarrassed as they realized I didn't work at the store my smile and the selfless act would hit them right in the insecurities, knowing they could have put their own cart away.

The age-old excuse many speak of, to include myself once upon a time, is the ever-so-common "I don't have the time." We all have the time. It's a matter of how we allocate that time and what's a priority for us. If you allocate your time and prioritize being a good human, you'll become one or improve upon what you already are.

Let's consider two very successful and very busy men, Jeff Bezos and Elon Musk. They're two of the wealthiest people walking this earth and we can assume they're swamped in their day-to-day activities. They have to prioritize their time and energy for what they see fit for accomplishing what they're focused on. I read that Bezos has his days so well planned that his email efforts account for less than five percent of his day, only answering emails in a block time that's well-planned. In contrast, the average business owner spends 20–40% of the day answering emails with no boundaries around the time frame.

As I'd look around the grocery store parking lot and study the humans and their behavior of leaving their carts behind, I came up with the idea that they weren't nearly as busy as I was. However, I allocate my time and priorities to be a good human.

Before we get ahead of ourselves, the assumption I came up with was based on studying people's clothing, the purse carried, how they carried themselves, the watch worn and car driven. Wealth recognizes wealth, and 99% of those I watched were not wealthy. I concluded they weren't busier than I, but were not correctly prioritizing their time to be a good human. Regardless of income level and success, if you want to be wealthy and successful, putting your shopping cart away is an excellent step in the right direction.

CREATING MOVEMENT, LEADING BY EXAMPLE

By no means will I take responsibility for the movement of being a good human; however, I continue to create a buzz around the movement, teaching others how to be a good human and leading by example as I go about my day. Many of my students from Warrior Consulting also do the same.

I didn't realize others might see me and follow suit as I put my carts away, though it's possible they did. But I know for sure that when I'd be taking pictures and video of me putting my carts away, and more notably, stopping and grabbing others carts that were left out and then post to socials, it would create a considerable discussion and then something significant would happen. I noticed my audience and followers started doing the same thing, taking videos and pictures of them putting their carts away, along with stopping and grabbing other carts and putting them away too. They'd tag me in the post and be proud of their selfless action.

I soon noticed other examples of people being good humans. What made it even better was that my audience started competing with each other to see who could grab the most shopping carts at once and wheel them back to where they needed to go.

A buddy of mine successfully took seven carts back at once while videoing himself and "winning" the competition. This was a proud moment for me, as the buzz around the movement started to get out and humans were becoming better. Social media is a tool; use it as a tool and you can create influence, connections, money, power, a business…and a movement.

PICK UP AFTER YOUR DOG

Here's more low-hanging fruit about being a good human. Walking your dog around your neighborhood, have you noticed how often you see a pile of dog poop? After many years of having dogs, walking them around where I live, in the woods or on vacations, there's a constant theme I come across: It's easy to separate yourself by cleaning up after your dog. Just keep a bag in your pocket, pull out the bag while your dog is relieving itself, reach down and clean up the mess that most just leave for the rest of us to step in.

Being a good human includes cleaning up after your dog, and also putting the mess in a trash can where it belongs. Maybe you're short on time and have a lot on your plate that day. I've counted the seconds—it's eight—seconds, not minutes it takes to pick and throw away the mess a dog leaves. I have to budget an extra 20 seconds of my day to account for the time it takes to be a good human by cleaning up after my dog. If we walk twice a day, that means less than one minute is budgeted to doing the right thing. And the best part is, you can do it too.

DON'T PEE ON THE SEAT

When I had a robust entity of over 60 employees who were primarily entry-level workers—mostly late teenage years and early to mid-20s—I'd often question myself with the age-old saying, "What the hell happened to America? Everyone is lazy."

But it wasn't a matter of those working for me being lazy; it was a matter of me holding myself to a higher standard than arguably 95 percent of Americans. I thought since I was taught when I was a child to clean up after myself to include in the bathroom, whether it was the water or hair around the sink, pee on the seat or anything to do with the toilet that goes out of hand, I assumed these lessons were taught to others too. I was wrong about that assumption.

We had locker rooms for our customers, but the majority of the staff all used one bathroom, and I saw just how little many cared to clean up after themselves—let alone do the right thing, be a good human and clean urine off the toilet seat when you're done using it.

I was alarmed at how often I'd clean up after others and then address the staff in a group setting because it was impossible to catch individual culprits in the act. I'd go on and on about how keeping the staff bathroom was important for the overall well-being and cleanliness of our team, how our female team members didn't want to sit in urine to use the bathroom, long-winded speeches about respect, which was one of our company core values—it was actually the top core value for our company. I'd speak about why it was so important for us as a team and them as team members to be a good human and clean up after themselves once done in the bathroom.

I was one of the few humans in that company who had the lesson of cleaning up after themselves beaten into them as children. I realized this when teaching a 20-something-year-old for the first time in his life that he should clean up after himself. It would fall upon deaf ears, as no matter what I did, taught, preached and encouraged, the result was typically the same.

This lesson further taught me early in my employer days that there's a lot of head nodding when the boss was around, but when the boss left, most people do what they were used to doing and or as little as needed to get by while keeping their entry-level job.

You have to carefully pick your audience when preaching anything, let alone how to be a good human. Fundamentally speaking, unsolicited advice often isn't taken and when I say often, I mean…usually never. On the other hand, when you pick your audience and the audience your message resonates with—those who support you and what you stand for—what you preach will not fall upon deaf ears.

Your family is a great example of an audience who supports you. Say you're in my mom's shoes beating me into submission to clean up after myself in the bathroom. You're the parent with a young impressionable son or daughter. Now, I'm by no means supporting hitting your child, as the way I was raised was unique yet very effective in the 1980s and '90s. Back then, it was a bit more socially acceptable to get a wooden spoon across the behind when you left urine on the bathroom seat with a mother and sister who despised it and acted as though the world was ending if they encountered it.

Your children can be the perfect audience to teach the basic fundamental lessons of cleaning up after themselves in the bathroom, and how important it is for this world to have good humans act selflessly in an environment where most are unknowingly selfish. Because you're a parent and your child brought into this world is learning and looks up to you, he or she will embody this lesson, just as you and I did growing up, wooden spoon or not.

There are exceptions of children who don't fall into the category of being the right audience to teach and pass on the lesson of being a good human. That's why there are other examples of other impressionable audiences, such as the person who asks you for advice. This person looks up to you and values your opinion. These are the people I pour my time and energy into preaching and teaching; they have open minds to hear what I'm teaching. You, too, can pass your lessons and advice along to those who seek advice from you.

Don't waste your time and energy on those who don't value or seek your advice. Teach all you can about how much this world needs more good humans.

Be a good human. End of the story.

PICKING UP THE TRASH

This topic hits home and is commonly the most performed act because it's an essential part of wholeheartedly embodying being a good human. It hit home for me because I see just how careless most humans are by letting their trash fall to the ground rather than taking the time to put their trash in a garbage can.

When you drive down the highway, let alone a smaller country road, if you pay attention, you'll notice how much trash is scattered on the side of the streets we travel on daily. It gets to me when I pull into a gas station and there's trash everywhere, often right around the actual trash can.

I clean up the trash whenever I see it, no matter where I am. Often while walking my dogs, I clean up trash near where I live even though my neighborhood is immaculate. I still grab loose pieces of trash as often as I can, put it in my pocket or extra poop bag and carry on with my day knowing I'm a good human.

Say I'm out to dinner at a restaurant or bar and go to the bathroom and see trash on the floor along with a pile of toilet paper. I bend down and pick it all up and throw it away where it belongs. I wash my hands after this, of course, but I want to let you in on a little secret. Earlier in the book, we discussed the principle that what we give is what we get, what we reap is what we sow, how we treat others is how we'll be treated—the universe is watching.

It often gives us little surprises, just as it does while I'm cleaning up trash. You'd be surprised how much money I find on the ground, especially at gas stations while picking up trash, not only loose change, but bills…often big bills. I teach this to my students and clients of Warrior Consulting and then they find money on the ground too, and lots of it. I don't want you to think we clean up trash for money; clean up trash to be a good human and the universe will see this selfless act and rightfully reward you as it sees fit.

The lesson here is to pick up trash and spend a few seconds helping humanity by being a good human. We don't do it for the money; we do it to leave the world a better place than it was when we woke up in the morning. Little acts such as cleaning up trash in a public bathroom or on the ground while filling up your car or walking your dog will go a long way in your life and in those lives you're surrounded by. You'll be impacting others, teaching them to do the right thing and leading by example.

TELL THE TRUTH

This one is self-explanatory: Lying isn't something a good human does. I'd never justify lying to anyone, and many people I know agree with the statement outside of possibly a harmless white lie to cover up something like a surprise. There's a fine line between being manipulative, deceitful or controlling and secretly doing something to make a loved one happy.

Having discipline in life will equate to how much success you find. A disciplined man or woman is someone who has self-control—self-control with their food, their diet, their fitness, their mindset, their job, their business, their physiological health and their ability to speak the truth even when their voice shakes and it's the last thing they want to do at that moment.

Speak the truth no matter how hard it might be, no matter how much you fear what you'll hear or see in response…no matter what.

Speaking the truth is a fundamental part of being a good human and is a successful human character trait. We'll all make mistakes when it comes to the truth and if a mistake was made, analyze the situation, admit fault, learn from it and put a plan in place to never again make that mistake with the truth.

DONATING

When I was a child, my mother always encouraged us to bag up clothing that no longer fit so we could donate it to others who were in need, preaching for us to be selfless and help others by lending them a helping hand when they need it.

As I grew up, I realized we were one of those families in need of a helping hand and hand-me-down clothing when we hit tough times after my father was diagnosed with cancer and couldn't work much. I was young enough at this point that I thought what we did was normal and that everyone bagged up and donated their clothing when it no longer fit. To me, my mom knew all and that what she said was right.

As time went on and our family struggled financially, I grew older and then came to the harsh reality of the world and the town I grew up in, which is the very wealthy Guilford, CT. It was my family who struggled, not other families.

Other families may have donated their clothing too; however, I began to realize it wasn't common practice and that other families looked down on us, or at least the kids did and would bully, make fun of and do what kids do by using our struggles as the brunt of their jokes.

I struggled greatly due to the flack I'd catch for being broke, so I turned to fighting and became very good at it, to the point where no one would fight me, other than a few occasions that didn't last too long.

Three decades later, I understand human psychology well enough that I understand why other families didn't donate, along with why kids liked to pick on us for being broke. An interesting point in life comes when you no longer get angry with people because you understand human psychology well enough.

When we have things in life, not limited to clothing that no longer fits, but anything that no longer serves us, it's a great practice to move them out of your life. I'm not telling you to close the door on people in your life; I'm saying there might be things and people in your life that no longer serve you, like a shirt that no longer fits or a couch that needs to be retired or that friend who isn't a friend—the one who takes from your time, energy and money.

Some people do all the taking and give nothing back.

These are examples of things in your life that no longer serve you and like the shirt that no longer fits, it's time to hand it down or donate it where the shirt will serve a purpose for someone in need, like when I was a boy and needed clothing that fit.

When we learn to release in our life what no longer serves us, we CREATE ROOM for things and people who will serve us and even things we want.

I've heard examples of people embarrassed by how old a suit was, who didn't feel confident showing up to a job interview, so they donated that suit and then the next day, a friend calls and asks what size they are because the suit they just bought doesn't fit right.

There have been situations I've watched my clients partake in or things they've done over the years that didn't align with our relationship and would violate our agreement. I'd have no other choice but to let them go to find their good elsewhere and then the PERFECT long-term client would appear out of what seemed like thin air, providing a relationship that's harmonious for years.

When we understand that the universe is watching our every move, listening to us and will give us what we ask for, we learn to operate with the mentality of "I GIVE UP AND TRUST the universe will deliver all I desire."

I desire to only work with students and clients where we

have a beautiful, progressive, positive and harmonious relationship that's great for both of us. If a client needs to be fired for doing something unethical, so be it. This makes room for the perfect client to find their way to me, and this will work for you too.

The same goes for your partner or romantic relationship. If the time comes where you have to move on, give up and trust that the universe will put the perfect person into your life at the perfect time.

We have to create room within ourselves and our surroundings by donating and clearing out things and people that no longer serve our highest and best good. By making room and clearing things out, we create the room for the perfect thing, object, event or person to come into our life at the perfect time.

Audit your circle of people HEAVILY and identify who is there only to take from you. If you want a sure-fire way to establish this, stop texting everyone. You'll see who reaches out and when they do, what they want then is a telltale sign of who is there only to take.

Clean out your closet of clothing you no longer wear. If you've recently lost weight and are feeling good yet still have your bigger clothing in the house, you are subconsciously aware the clothing is there. You know you can put it on if you get bigger again. Clean it all out, all seasons and donate it to a friend or family member, or to a random place that accepts donations, such as Goodwill or The Salvation Army. This will create room for better clothing to come into your life.

Do this regardless of the price you paid. If you wear high-end clothing, donate it just like you would a used pair of pants as it will serve someone else. I've donated a $1,500 tailored Hugo Boss suit because it no longer served me; rather than trying to recoup money out of it by selling, I knew someone would fall in love with it and it would make his day.

You know that junk drawer in your house? Or maybe that junk room? Maybe the garage? Anything that no longer serves you and sits there collecting dust can find a new home; someone will appreciate it being in their life more than most of us can conceptualize.

When I was in the military, I was young, but while traveling the world, specifically very poor countries in the Middle East, I saw people killing one another for necessities, things you and I take for granted, just throwing it away when we're done with it. I wish this wasn't reality; however, poor, war-torn third-world countries seemed to be another world at times.

Bridging back to cleaning out your closet, drawer, room, garage or house, the more, the merrier, and do it often. For example, I often look through my wardrobe of shirts that are too big, shorts that no longer fit well, pants that are tight or loose, shoes that are worn, jackets I'm swimming in, or anything that's no longer in style. I bag them up, just as my mother taught me three decades ago, and drive them to the nearest donation site unless I have someone specifically in mind who would benefit from them. This practice has created room for a beautiful, high-end wardrobe that fits well and about which I often receive compliments.

Regardless of price tag, quality or abundance of clothing, the principle of creating room for good to come into your life is the important part. We all have a starting point, growing from there into whatever you desire. You get what you give; you receive what you're vibrationally aligned to; the universe sees every move you make, hears everything you ask for and will put things into your life at exactly the right time. We reap what we sow—now create all the room for the good by giving first as a good human.

HELPING OTHERS

As you're now realizing, being a good human is much more than just putting your shopping cart away when you're done with it, even though putting your shopping cart away is a fundamental act of selflessness and is part of being a good, disciplined human.

There are many layers to becoming and embodying being a good human, so much so that in one of my companies, I put together a bonus every month to any member of the team who displayed what I called "Going above and beyond." Every month, we'd hear a story from one of our team members who went out of their way to be an amazing human, doing an act of service to help another human. Once we deemed the award winner, the person would receive whatever their sales commission was for that month or if they weren't in a sales role, their paycheck plus an additional 20 percent of their pay.

I always knew which new hires read the employee manual because they'd be in the running for the award the first month. They came on board and it was easy to separate themselves from the rest of the pack when we brought on several new hires at once. Those were the new employees I watched closely as they were many things, including well-read and money-driven. Being money-driven is common and arguably the root to why most have become successful in life, which is to have financial gain.

When talking about late teen and early 20-year-old new hires who are money-driven, the real piece to the pie was WHY they're money-driven. Was it for themselves, to help support their family, girlfriend, boyfriend, wife or husband? Once I figured out why they were money-driven, I'd watch closely to see if their actions to collect more was pure.

Most people, including newly hired employees, think impressing the owner is a good thing. I agree with the statement; however, I offer a different perspective. The number of times my company was stolen from through internal theft was in the dozens, and it was always from those who specifically tried to impress me.

Human nature is inherently selfish, which I'd learned by observation. This would be one of the reasons I'd watch closely who won the "above and beyond" award. I wouldn't expect to be stolen from after I handed out the award. However, I knew it was possible from the money-driven person. I was trying to create a culture of selfless, good humans who would be rewarded for going above and beyond their job and showing the community a great example of those working for us.

For the most part, it did and a lot of the stories of those I passed the awards out to were nothing short of amazing. Oddly, those were some of the people who fabricated stories to win the award or took product or money from the company.

As for the stories of the award and its winners, one of the best stories I heard from my managers was of one of our newer and younger team members going above and beyond to help another team member. We'll call her Susan, who had been teaching yoga for upward of 40 years, including for me.

Unbeknownst to most of us, Susan's husband was very sick with cancer, and both she and her husband were on the older side, nearing late 60s or even 70s. There had been a snowstorm one day and someone on our team went food shopping for them and also shoveled the driveway and walkways for them, put the food away and cooked them dinner because Susan wasn't physically capable of much after taking care of her husband. This story didn't take place due to our award. This story took place because of someone being a good human and genuinely wanting to care for other humans in need.

There will always be a time when people require a helping hand. The difference between a normal person and a good human is when we put others first and lend the helping hand they so desperately need. Focus on helping others when THEY need help, not when it's convenient for you. That's the key to wholeheartedly being a great human.

Here are other examples to help drive home the selfless acts it takes to embody helping others. I'd just had surgery on my chest and had strict orders from my doctor not to work out; I wasn't even allowed to walk my dog. The surgeon wanted my upper body motionless to allow the healing process to take place. That was understandable because even putting on or taking off my shirt, opening or closing doors or driving was discomforting and painful; I often needed help undressing.

This was the state I was in, on mild pain killers and operating four companies. I'd just hired an assistant that week, so in my usual fashion, I decided to onboard her and do some work the day after surgery. I needed to go out and she offered to drive, which was a lifesaver given the situation. It was a very windy day, windy to the point I saw my neighbors trash cans in the road and, against my best judgment, I grabbed them and put them away.

As the day went on, I told my newly hired assistant to pull over to the side of the road; she was confused and thought she'd done something wrong. I could tell she was nervous, but I was about to teach her how to help others when they need help, no matter if it's convenient for you or not, as in most cases.

We were driving down Route One in Milford, Connecticut; most accidents in the state happen on this road and, low and behold, I saw a couple of trash cans in the middle of a four-lane road. I got out of the car, which was painful having had surgery less than 24 hours prior, walked into the oncoming traffic to collect the trash cans, drug them back to the side of the road and put them someplace safer.

It was a perfect time and perfect example to teach my new hire what above and beyond looks like, how to act selflessly and how to be a good human from day one. My belief is to lead from the front, lead by example and to show people in your life how it's done, long before you ask them to do the same. When you take the approach of leading by example, say teaching your children, they'll trust you more as they see you stepping up first and providing them a safe environment to learn the lesson you're teaching.

Several months after the trash can event she and I were on our way to a recording of my show The CW Clinic found on all major platforms, iTunes, Spotify, YouTube or all major podcast broadcasting channels) in the dead of winter with the temperature hovering around 20 degrees.

Regardless that I had to meet a team to record my show or that it was cold, I saw someone in need. We were at a tight four-way intersection at a railroad overcrossing and I noticed an

18-wheeler truck attempting to make it under the bridge—he wasn't going to make it. I pulled up to him from the opposite direction and tried to wave him down before he hit his roof, but I was too late. I got out of my car and we talked about how to get out of the situation. We decided it was best to put the truck in reverse and back out.

Once we agreed on the plan, I stayed in the road so on-coming traffic wouldn't approach. I waved and yelled at the cars behind him to move, which was a tough task as the roads were tight and there wasn't much room to maneuver a car, let alone a semi. He backed out from under the bridge with what looked to be minimal damage, so I drove ahead and blocked off the road so he'd have a clear path to back up and exit, which he did.

I didn't know who he was, what company he worked for, but I knew by the look on his face that he was scared and angry. It was the least I could do to help him and ease his stress a bit, because someone on the ground directing traffic was a huge help. I never caught his name, but I did catch the smile on his face when he was able to get out of the situation, and that made it all worth it.

I'm a huge fan of winter. I've been an avid snowboarder for close to 30 years and am a big-time day hiker, so I find myself in situations of driving in Nor'easters and heavy snowstorms as I chase them for pleasure. When heavy snowfalls come, many people don't have proper tires and think they can drive in snow and in storms. This is a perfect recipe for sliding off the road or flipping and worse accidents.

I became so used to this, I started carrying tow straps, shovels, extra gloves and jumper cables to be the good human who pulls over to help people in their time of need. It's fun to help dig people out and then take the time to educate them about tires being the reason for the problem—not the car, which most people don't grasp until someone explains it.

The number of cars I've helped out is too many to count, but the real fun is hooking up a tow strap to your winter sports car and banging through some gears to pull out cars and trucks from ditches.

One time I threw a big New Year's Eve party at my house in Vermont with lots of my favorite friends. The plan was to wake up super early and catch the first chairlift going up the hill on New Year's Day. My friends and I were planning on this, but also enjoyed playing games and drinking champagne to welcome the new year as we were all beginning to do well in life and having fun doing so.

At one point, a couple of the girlfriends started arguing, and it got to the point that a grad school buddy of mine who had recently tried out for the NFL decided he'd take his girlfriend out of the situation because things were heating up. I urged him not to leave, as not only were we on a remote mountain, it was snowing heavily and had been for days. And, don't forget, it was New Year's Eve. Against my better judgment, I let him leave and he said he'd meet up with us the next day on the hill to take some turns.

The night went on, champagne was consumed, games were played and the new year was welcomed. We woke up early to get to the mountain to catch the first chairlift headed up the hill. To our amazement considering the festivities the night prior, we woke up in good shape, cooked up a hardy breakfast accompanied with mimosas ushering in the new year around 5:00 a.m. We loaded up my car and headed out, as we knew it would be an amazing day on the hill given the copious amounts of snow that had fallen that night.

On our way down the hill, I was taking it slow. I've learned that while driving downhill in the mountains, if an accident is going to happen, it's in the downhill direction. Up is for playing in the snow and drifting.

Anyway, there was a sharp turn coming up; I was slowing down as I was going into the turn and saw what looked like a car in the ditch. I stopped my car, got out and saw the car was my friend's. He and his girlfriend were passed out; the car was still on and the heat was pumping to keep them warm.

Fortunately, a friend in my car was a city police officer, had experienced this situation often and was ready to help. We woke our friends and got ready to pull the car out of the ditch with my tow strap. At the time, I was driving a Subaru STI with proper winter tires and some engine work done, which meant it was prime for ripping cars out of ditches with a foot or more of snow on the ground.

And so we did; we pulled him out, unhooked the strap and raced toward the mountain to catch the first chairlift going up the hill. Even after stopping to pull them out of the ditch, we still made it to the first chair, mimosas in hand and so started a New Year's tradition I've taken part in for many years.

I hope these stories articulate the message that being a good human isn't only life-changing, but can be fun when you're genuinely selfless and caring for other people as you want to see them do well in a time of need. As we near the end of this chapter, we'll close with the last section of being a good human, with the core principle that makes us embody the action of movement of being a good human: discipline.

DISCIPLINE

When I accepted discipline for the first time after entering the Army, I suddenly had drill sergeants yelling in my face, plus all the psychological warfare they play. I had no choice; I had to conform to discipline or my day would fall apart into pieces fast.

When you get to boot camp, your entire world is turned upside down. Everything you know is no longer, so you give up and don't fight back.

At least, we smart ones made that decision—those who fought back were exercised until they were broken or punished and embarrassed to the degree they'd cry out about wanting to kill themselves because that's the only way out of the torment. That was the reality of not accepting all you were told, to include discipline and the seven Army core values. The seven Army core values all had discipline intertwined within them, starting with loyalty.

Let's take a look at those core values for perspective and understanding how discipline played a significant role in my life. It was forced upon me, and I'm a grateful man, all these years after that glorious day I showed up at Ft. Benning, GA, home of the Infantry boot camp and Advanced Individual Training.

LOYALTY

Bear true faith and allegiance to the U.S. Constitution, the Army, your unit and other soldiers. Bearing true faith and allegiance is a matter of believing in and devoting yourself to something or someone. A loyal Soldier is one who supports the leadership and stands up for fellow soldiers. By wearing the uniform of the U.S. Army, you're expressing your loyalty. And by doing your share, you show your loyalty to your unit.

DUTY

Fulfill your obligations. Doing your duty means more than carrying out your assigned tasks. Duty means being able to accomplish tasks as part of a team. The work of the U.S. Army is a complex combination of missions, tasks, and responsibilities—all in constant motion. Our work entails building one assignment onto another. You fulfill your obligations as a part of your unit every time you resist the temptation to take "shortcuts" that might undermine the integrity of the final product.

RESPECT

Treat people as they should be treated. In the Soldier's Code, we pledge to "treat others with dignity and respect while expecting others to do the same." Respect is what allows us to appreciate the best in other people. Respect is trusting that all people have done their jobs and fulfilled their duty. And self-respect is a vital ingredient with the Army value of respect, which results from knowing you've put forth your best effort. The Army is one team, and each of us has something to contribute.

SELFLESS SERVICE

Put the welfare of the Nation, the Army, and your subordinates before your own. Selfless service is larger than just one person. In serving your country, you're doing your duty loyally without thought of recognition or gain. The basic building block of selfless service is the commitment of each team member to go a little further, endure a little longer, and look a little closer to see how he or she can add to the effort.

HONOR

Live up to Army values. The Nation's highest military award is The Medal of Honor. This award goes to soldiers who make honor a matter of daily living—soldiers who develop the habit of being honorable and solidify that habit with every value choice they make. Honor is a matter of carrying out, acting, and living the values of respect, duty, loyalty, selfless service, integrity, and personal courage in everything you do.

INTEGRITY

Do what's right, legally and morally. Integrity is a quality you develop by adhering to moral principles. It requires that you do and say nothing that deceives others. As your integrity grows, so does the trust others place in you. The more choices you make based on integrity, the more this highly prized value will affect your relationships with family and friends, and, finally, the fundamental acceptance of yourself.

PERSONAL COURAGE

Face fear, danger, or adversity (physical or moral). Personal courage has long been associated with our Army. With physical courage, it's a matter of enduring physical duress and, at times, risking personal safety. Facing mortal fear or adversity may be a long, slow process of continuing forward on the right path, especially if taking those actions isn't popular with others. You can build your personal courage by daily standing up for and acting upon the things you know are honorable.

For a full history of the US Army Core Values, go to:
https://caccapl.blob.core.usgovcloudapi.net/web/character-development-project/repository/a-brief-history-of-the-army-values.pdf

These core values play a huge role in my life and always

will. They were forced upon me—I had no choice but to accept them. As time went on, I developed core values for my companies to embody. We understand our core values for one another, our customers, our clients, our audience and ourselves.

When I first thought about making core values for my companies, I didn't know where to start. However, I knew it needed to be done for the greater good of everyone working with me. I brought my managers together to discuss a mastermind group. A mastermind group is where everyone in the group is there to achieve the same mission harmoniously together.

I challenged them to help develop the core values as I searched the depths of my life for what I thought would be fair for all. I started with the core values gained when I was 19. As my team worked on what they felt were our core values, I thought of the two values that spoke to me most from the Army that related to a civilian business: respect and selflessness. Both respect and selflessness have the principle of discipline and would help the staff embody being great humans, and they often did.

It's ironic because discipline was not a new topic for me to conceptualize as a kid, nor was it the first time I heard of it when the Army demanded it from me as a young soldier. As a kid growing up under my father, who also served in the military during the Vietnam era, I was taught discipline from an early age. My mother instilled discipline also, but my father demanded it from me on the sports field as my coach and off and on throughout life.

He taught me by having me cutting the lawn, shoveling snow, splitting, stacking and moving wood for our wood-burning stove and other chores around the house most kids under the age of 10 weren't doing. I was paid a small allowance to accomplish these tasks, which kept me disciplined enough to achieve them.

However, when he became sick with cancer in the early 1990s, for some odd reason I rebelled being required to do anything. In hindsight, it's simple to understand what I didn't know then: I was angry that my father was sick, which heavily affected our family.

Discipline went out the window over the next 10 years, as I was constantly getting into trouble in and out of school, run-ins with the police, suspensions from school, often fighting anyone who would fight me back. It wasn't the prettiest sight. Still, neither is watching your father die, as you can probably understand. Discipline went out the window from about age seven to 19, when boot camp changed things VERY quickly.

DISCIPLINE AS LIFE GOES ON

Then an interesting thing happened. Suddenly, discipline played a huge part in my life. I had no choice. When the day came that it was my choice whether or not to keep discipline in life, I kept it and then, unknowingly through my first era of expertise, fitness, began to teach others how to adapt the core value of discipline. At that time, I didn't have a clue my purpose on this earth was to teach others, but I did know I wanted more out of life and couldn't let an undisciplined childhood dictate where the next few decades would go.

When I made the transition out of the military, I kept my physical shape and health as a top priority. I went back to school and added schooling into the discipline mix. I buckled down and kept straight As, maintained an incredible physique and then started training others, teaching them what I'd learned in the hope they'd adopt discipline in their lives through the application of fitness.

As time went on, I started dreaming of wanting to achieve bigger things in life, things most of, if not everyone in my life thought I was crazy to talk about.

Pro Tip: If people in your life tell you what you're dreaming of is crazy, it's time to audit your circle of who you're listening to. Go to *chriswarnes.com,* select the podcast tab and look for Episode 6, "Auditing Your Circle" to discover how to be around an amazing group of people.

Dreams scared me; however, I knew I could accomplish whatever I dreamed of through hard work. Discipline played an integral part in success and wealth, which I found early in life; discipline is also why the dreams others thought were crazy were accomplished. I dreamed of owning sports cars and motorcycles, starting a business, competing in the fitness field, buying a home and making $10,000 a month, all of which was accomplished by my mid-20s. I dreamed of going to grad school and opening a second business—a full-service gym—both complete by my early 30s. Discipline got me there.

I dreamed of leading a large staff, working with and mentoring the team, having thousands of customers, along with helping teach them how to accomplish their fitness goals and then crossing the seven-figure annually mark, and so I did. Discipline got me there.

I dreamed of building a podcast, opening a third, fourth and fifth company, working with students teaching them how to live a successful life and operating prosperous businesses for themselves. Discipline got me there.

I dreamed of writing a book and a whole slew of other things and discipline got me there too. Discipline is an underrated core value that's fundamental in life, success, networking, health, building wealth and accomplishing anything you dream of.

Now we'll discuss how you can build anything, any life, any dream you dream of by channeling discipline.

DISCIPLINE AGAIN

You too can achieve whatever you desire, no matter how outlandish or far-fetched you may think your dreams are. You have permission to do everything in your power, day in and day out, to accomplish them.

With the daily application of discipline in your habits—embodying discipline—you will achieve all you desire. If you want something badly enough, badly enough you'd rather die than take another step forward in life, write down your dream and put it somewhere you'll see it daily.

On the screen saver of your phone, the screen of your laptop, the mirror in the bathroom, on your refrigerator—let these goals stare you down. Look at them daily.

Build a vision board; take the time to hang it somewhere you'll see daily. You can accomplish anything you desire... ANYTHING you can see on the screen of your mind, you can hold in your hand. Discipline can help get you to all you desire, all you dream of, all you KNOW you can accomplish.

I know you can do it, and more importantly, you know you can do it. Winning and winning together is what makes a thriving community. We, as good humans, can and will prevail.

YOU'LL WIN. WE'LL WIN.

CHAPTER 7

WHEN TO LET GO

This chapter wasn't originally in the plan for this book or the live system I teach. In March of 2020 when I officially opened the doors for students to learn from me, I designed this course with only six modules to teach live, and when I began writing this book, I'd only planned six chapters.

But the universe will give you signs all the time. The key difference between most people is that very few have the belief system or capacity to recognize these signs. How I advocate learning to recognize signs from the universe is exactly how I teach through meditation and connecting yourself to a source or higher power. Once you do, you'll get signs all the time, sometimes when you're least expecting it and often when you're not in the mood to receive them.

Initially, it's similar to kicking the beehive and can be uncomfortable. When you open yourself up to a higher power of the universe, always knowing what you want to receive, you're asking for it. Then, receiving the signs from the universe, we learn to follow these signs, downloads and plans.

Before we discuss what to do once we get signs from the universe, let's talk about "downloads." Downloads are when you get a serious amount of information coming your way—we're talking about a plethora of information, like… *all the information.*

I'll give you an example of a monster download I had in 2020. In August of 2020, I was sitting at my kitchen table talking to my then-girlfriend, accepting that the 1% rule applied to my situation in life, and I would have to close a business, which was difficult to swallow, mostly because I did absolutely nothing to bring on the situation.

I was talking through the situation and suddenly had a crippling sensation come over me, my skin tightening to the point it hurt…and I went blank. Since returning home from war, the number of times "I've left a conversation," staring into thin air or out a window for minutes on end is too often to count as my mind took me back to war or a specific event I experienced. This was different.

We're not talking about that blank look where we just stare into space; we're talking about images coming into my mind—fast, ideas, thoughts, images, images of people or things talking to me. I'm aware this might sound odd and until you open yourself up for this to happen, it won't. It won't happen until you decide to "give up and trust" that what will be will be and the universe supplies you with a plan and that when you receive the plan, you'll follow it tirelessly.

With tireless practice and discipline, you'll get to this point one day, some faster than others. When it does happen, it will be the answers you've been searching for, the answers you've always known subconsciously, but now the plan has been provided.

These answers will be provided in the form of a download. Downloads are the real deal, and I encourage all my students to embrace them.

Only moments prior to this particular download, I was questioning my entire existence, why I was on this earth in this lifetime and what the future of this life held for me. I was slipping into a negative mindset and was working harder than I ever had in my life to reframe the situation so I could stay positive.

Suddenly, it happened; I got up, grabbed my notebook and pen and began writing everything coming to my mind, and there was a lot. This download contained all the answers I had been looking for.

With no warning, a five-year plan for myself, my relationships and my businesses just came to me…in detail—scary detail, vivid detail, cycles, patterns, cross pollinations, promotions, platforms, marketing campaigns, bundles, packages, books, politics, speaking events, international travel, the team, homes, cars…EVERYTHING.

I didn't time the event; however, I know it lasted a couple hours, if not more. The conversation was mid-morning on the weekend and by the time the download was complete, I looked at my watch and it was early afternoon.

WHAT TO DO WHEN YOU RECEIVE THE SIGNS

When you start to receive signs from a source, subconscious or our higher self, it's imperative to write these signs down. Think about it this way, how often do you say to yourself, "Wow, I had such a great idea, but I forgot it"?

We have lots of signs, downloads and ideas throughout the day and we'll never remember them all—it's impossible to remember everything. Write them down.

It's not important to execute the sign that very moment; in fact, it's usually not possible. Build systems to review anything you write. For instance, I have two notebooks and a handwritten schedule. Once a week, I review everything I write down in each notebook to review all the ideas, signs and downloads that come to me throughout the week so I can schedule or delegate them.

The universe and your higher self will provide you with the answers to the questions you have and all you ask for, so be very clear about what you want and all you ask for. You can and will manifest anything in your life, good or bad. After you receive the signs and build a system to unpack them whether it's in the moment or afterward as I do, it comes down to what you'll actually do with the signs.

I believe so strongly in signs that one of my two notebooks is tiny and I always keep it on me to write down any nudge I get. All the planning of these nudges and signs has worked out VERY well for me, to include that monster download of a five-year plan.

For myself, along with many others who are successful with the law of attraction, our nudges, signs, downloads and plans have worked out well for us. They're the answers to all we desire and ask for.

Only when we give up and trust are we aligned and then ready to receive. Once we receive, it's on us, as it's on you to execute the action of acting upon the answers you receive. If we can do it, you can do it too.

If you don't believe you can do it, the following are a few stories of my students and me. You'll see how we've used these signs to know when it's time to let go of what was holding us back in life.

TOXIC RELATIONSHIPS

There will be an exception to this, the one percent who may not have had a toxic romantic relationship. That might be you and if so, I commend you. However, most of us go through these relationships to learn what isn't aligned to us and further prove to ourselves what we don't need in our lives to live purposefully and harmoniously. Relationships are similar to going to a Baskin-Robbins; you get there, try different flavors and you might find a flavor that doesn't agree with you, which is similar to a toxic relationship.

In my late 20s, I'd bought a house, was driving a new car, had built my first business, crossed the six-figure mark financially and was getting a lot of attention from people I knew, on and offline. Things were going well; I was growing, my clients were winning fitness shows, earning pro cards—I was changing people's lives through healthy lifestyle coaching and was building momentum in life.

I started seeing a girl I'd coached for fitness shows. She expressed interest in seeing each other and so we did. Things went well; she was stunningly beautiful, with long dark hair, olive skin, a fit and well-built body, which was exactly my type, so we started dating.

Early in the relationship, less than six months in, I discovered she was lying about things, which should have been a red flag to be cautious or exit the relationship. However, like the patient young man I was, I gave her the benefit of the doubt. Where I went wrong was continuing to give the benefit of the doubt through the entire relationship. I was intoxicated with beauty rather than substance, depth or character, which are fundamental factors upon which good, healthy and long-lasting relationships are founded.

The entire situation was my fault, and I'm completely to blame as I lacked the ability to trust myself and my boundaries, and also lacked the ability to set expectations and boundaries with her due to my lack of ability to trust in myself.

As time went on, things only got worse. I was driven to open a gym, as well as enter and complete grad school, all while continuing to build the current company. I was laser focused, confident, dedicated and driven with a purpose to win and grow. I thought that with time, the things in the relationship would get better, thinking that time would work things out. I was stunningly wrong.

Time only brought more problems, including break-ups, getting back together, harsh words, tough arguments, negativity and bad energy between us, but I stayed locked on my vision.

I entered and completed grad school, traveled the country with her looking for gyms to buy and was thinking about moving out of state together, finding a gym in Connecticut where I'm from, negotiating and closing on it. I was growing my start-up business then too, changing lives and pumping out pro athletes like candy.

At that time in my coaching career, we brought a huge crew of athletes to fitness shows and occasionally had winners of almost every class on stage with complete domination of the show—boy, did we turn heads with our winnings.

Once I'd gotten to the point of having two companies and dozen of employees, I made the decision to bring the girlfriend into both my companies as the number two reporting directly to me. There was no paperwork or contract signed, only verbal discussions of rules and expectations.

One topic I discussed and would never sway in my thinking

was that I won't have a business partner—and this holds true to this day.

Our personal relationship was already rocky, and it continued to slide downhill.

Letting go of worn-out things, worn-out situations and worn-out relationships in life is a fundamental practice that has to be put into place to respect and trust ourselves as we grow through life. Regardless of age, the sooner you learn this lesson, the sooner you'll free yourself from people, things, events and situations that are no longer aligned with you.

About a year after opening the place, I vividly remember driving to Vermont for her birthday after a long workday of 12 hours. We got there, unpacked and I lay down, exhausted. It was the night before her birthday, and I just wanted her to be happy.

Shortly after lying down, she told me she wanted to talk and proceeded to tell me she hated me. The feeling of disappointment and rejection ran through me. Her statement was made not in anger in an argument, but was the pure truth.

We decided to stay together, which was again my fault. Shortly thereafter, on Valentine's Day, she asked, "What are we?" and I responded with the typical things a decent boyfriend would say to someone he thinks he loves.

I didn't realize she was asking if we were partners in the business and for possibly for the first time in the entire relationship spanning nearly five years, I stayed true to my word about partners and, my boundaries. My word as she propositioned me for partnership: No.

That didn't go over too well.

Here's an interesting thing about people: If you want to see where you stand with them, tell them no, and the true colors will come out quickly.

In my case, you can call that evening a coloring book.

"Selfish people make my skin crawl, the feeling's inescapable
They're anxious, if you're stuck in the mud, they won't wait for you
You're the only one that truly has your back
Tell a person no, watch how they react

Spoiled brats get mad, quickly throw a tantrum
Never let them in, they hold emotions for ransom."
~ Craig G
(From Limelight, used with permission)

Regardless, I still didn't let go. I've always had the protector and fixer mentality and still do to this day. However, my expectations, trusting myself and boundaries with myself and others is now far more advanced.

If I had to guess what was running through my mind at the time, it was probably optimism. My mindset was focused on personal and professional growth and my thoughts were predominately optimistic. I must have thought things would get better on their own, even after all the events that had unfolded.

Letting go when you're crippled by fear of the unknown, fear of abandonment, fear of judgment and fear of making the wrong decision all stand in the way of letting go. Fear is only an emotion; emotions can be understood with study as there are thousands of years of literature written about emotion and how to understand and step aside from emotion. Go to YouTube and search "Chris Warnes How to Conquer Fear" for more education about defeating your fears.

Fear of the unknown on the other side was undoubtedly what held me from letting go. Shortly thereafter, we broke up and I terminated her from both companies, after which I felt like a thousand pounds of brick was taken off my chest and another thousand cinderblocks released from my feet.

Isn't it ironic only in the end of toxic relationships do we see others for who they are through the actions they provide us with in the end?

Eventually, the conclusion was clear: I was responsible for it all. It was my responsibility because I only played myself the entire time. All I wanted was her beauty and all she wanted was the root of most greed and is easily spotted: the good old greenbacks, money.

"I keep pushing 'cause time never slows down
Only moves forward so be equipped with the know-how
To read people deep under their layers
Or be a human stepping stone, the answer to their prayers
Some work on a life that people see in the public
But never on their personal demons, they skip the subject
So they feel like the toast of the town
Smiling for the cameras at home, they feeling down
Their whole life is cosmetic, pathetic
Plastic like arms and legs that are prosthetic
Images are temporary, structures only make shift
Do yourself a favor and stay away from the fake shit"

~ Craig G
(From Limelight, used with permission)

Knowing when to let go was learned, and some of us must learn our lessons the hard way. We sometimes also need to repeatedly drive home how much we need to trust ourselves, our decisions, our intuition and, above all, trust what's best for us and our families over the long term. There's a silver lining that comes from learning lessons the hard way; it's all in how we look at the tough lessons and situations.

We have to keep the positive mindset and lens of focus on the situations after they're complete and the lessons are learned and, more importantly, during the process of learning when it's time to let go. The rocky road of struggle will lead you to all you desire as you're confronting the shortcoming in your life to inevitably grow with less weight around your ankles.

I taught an especially tough lesson to one of my first students, LJ, who had no clue he was being stolen from—not by his employees, but by his bosses.

Once we identified, confirmed and re-confirmed the truth, he recognized he was being robbed by the men who signed his checks. The especially hard part was teaching him it was time to let go. He'd just finished his first group course with me and a dozen other students, which gave him a new lease on life with a new mindset to tackle his days.

He thought so highly of the material I provided that he decided to hire me for some intensive one-on-one mentorship and business consulting to kick him into high gear. He was adapting the ethics, morals, values and mindset of the highest level and performing at the highest level as any student open to doing the work on themselves will once taking the leap and working with Warrior Consulting.

It's fair to point out that LJ and I went back several years—I was originally his customer; he was a referral when I owned a few tanning beds and needed them serviced. I reached out to a few friends and within the week, I met LJ, who is a kind, big-hearted, passionate and charismatic man of high intelligence. He's family-oriented and, although he didn't know at the time, was put on this earth to help and teach other humans.

As time went on, I needed more service and made sure I was present while he was working on my tanning beds, which was rare given my schedule and the number of laborers I had working for me. Something was different with him—his energy was powerful and aura was bright and clear.

We formed a friendship and things grew from there. He called me for life and business advice as he was self-employed too. This was long before I was formally teaching students other than my friends, family and a robust staff, but I enjoyed coaching him and giving back. LJ was thinking through the idea of giving up the self-employed life because his job had him traveling, often spending time out of state and away from his family with a newborn at home.

He was feeling guilty and was then presented with an opportunity. The opportunity was his competition, who offered him a job. They presented an appealing offer because they knew he was tired of traveling and wanted more time at home with his family. With good pay, incentives and structure, they had his attention. After a few calls back and forth, he asked what I thought about the proposal and my advice to him was, "Only do what is best for you and your family. And if that's with them, so be it."

He decided to take the job, and we then negotiated his contract and struck a great deal with him being paid what he wanted and had more time home with his young family. After about a year, I told him I was formally taking on clients and students to work with as I was launching my fifth company, Warrior Consulting. I was finally living the life I desired and wanted to execute being aligned with my life's purpose as a teacher.

I then offered him a spot in our first group program and without hesitation he said, "Yes, I want in. Send me the bill," with no questions asked. Fast forward to him completing the group program and wanting to work together more, hiring me for one-on-one mentor and business consulting because I blew his mind in the group setting.

We began to dive into his life and pick apart some blocks I noticed, which was tough to start with because most people hide from uncomfortable confrontation. Almost by accident, we stumbled upon a topic that, while he didn't know it at the time, was about to change his life.

We were focused on his personal life, past and blocks, and were not spending too much time on his career. However, one day he mentioned his bosses weren't paying him his commissions correctly, nor had he seen his profit-sharing bonus other than once. The bonuses were to be issued monthly per their agreement to bring LJ on as a partner. We had negotiated this in his contract.

Then, one statement threw up a massive red flag, and I went deep to figure out what was going on, having him gather the company's profit and loss statements, income statements and balance sheets. What I found was mind-blowing. We found money laundering, and his bosses weren't paying him, including upward of $60,000 on the conservative side, through lack of profit sharing and bonuses over the course of nine months of employment.

It was tough information to deliver, but that's my job, to deliver the truth hopefully in a manner that's received well. He did handle it well, and I advised him how to deal with the situation by addressing his bosses and also having the proper legal representation for a potential lawsuit in the worst-case scenario.

This is the point in the situation where focusing and being transparent that if the missing money was anything other than a mistake and everything isn't rectified between both parties, it's time to quickly let go.

Many people have such big hearts, we like to give people the benefit of the doubt. The key to this practice is to give the benefit of the doubt just once, not so many times that you can no longer keep count. People make mistakes. The type of human you are will speak volumes about your character when you deal with mistakes being made by others, especially mistakes that cost money, in this case $60,000.

LJ didn't want to face his bosses; he was nervous and didn't want to deal with it. His passive aggressive nature wanted to come out because he didn't like conflict in the slightest. Of course, there are ways to have the situation addressed by an attorney speaking on behalf of a client.

However, I advised him not to take that route but instead, to sit his bosses down, giving them the benefit of the doubt while presenting the facts we'd come up with and then going from there depending on their reaction. With good coaching and a support channel in place, LJ addressed his bosses man to man and received unprofessionalism and pushback.

This is the point where knowing when to let go of a situation is critical. Good coaches and mentors are able to guide their students through situations of all kinds. A great coach or mentor has been through difficult situations and knows what it takes and how hard it is to go through difficult situations.

LETTING GO WHEN IT COMES TO BUSINESS

The lessons from which we learn the most often bring along with them the most pain. That pain isn't always physical.

Physical pain correlated to lessons may be the easiest and quickest pain to learn from. The pain I've experienced is no greater than yours; pain is relative. Pain that feels like a lot to me, you may feel isn't much and pain I feel is low you may think is a lot. There's no right or wrong other than not allowing pain to swallow you up and ruin the rest of your life. The difference between failure and defeat is that fine line of getting back up, dusting yourself off and getting back after it.

That's life. You'll prevail.

In 2016, my life drastically changed as I was now a young full-service gym owner living my life's dream. I was on cloud nine. Gym ownership is challenging work, a very tough job; it never ends—it's around the clock. You wear all the hats from janitor to CEO and have to hold a smile while doing so.

I was never afraid of hard work that continued to come at me daily. But I did fear failure, which helped fuel me. The first year of ownership was more or less learning how to be a gym owner. If you're a hands-on guy like me, leading from the front requires an immense amount of energy. I made a lot of mistakes over my career, more than I cared to admit at the time. I admit them now, but the first year as an owner came with daily mistakes, if not multiple times a day. I made my mistakes and took my lessons with a smile as I typically wouldn't make those mistakes again.

However, by the end of the first year of ownership, I knew deep down that after eight years of self-employed hard work and the prior five years of military service, I didn't want to be an owner the rest of my life.

It's an odd feeling when you achieve what most would consider great success in many different departments in life, to be looked up to as a role model, to help others believe they can achieve all they desire and then look yourself in the mirror a year later and know the climb in the fitness industry was going to be short-lived.

I accepted the lesson, and it taught me how to work for something I knew was not aligned with my life path. This was the biggest lesson on selflessness I'd encountered since separating from the military and boy, did the work continue.

If you come to the same crossroad in life—achieving your dream and realizing it isn't for you—know that not only can it be expected, but many have gone through it before you. Discovering this can save your life if you find yourself in this position.

I continued to practice a lot of the skills I hadn't mastered. I had a lot to learn and a lot of resources to learn from. For example, I knew nothing about recruiting staff and decided to learn by teaching myself. In the beginning, I believed what job applicants said and trusted their words. How wrong that was, and that was one of the most expensive lessons I learned by trial and error.

Here are two great rules to live by when learning to employ and recruit.

Actions speak louder than words—so simple, yet so true. This applies to all areas of life to include romantic relationships; however, our lens of focus is hiring talent or the lack thereof. The amount you'll be told during recruiting and what's later under-delivered is incredible.

It's not that you're being lied to, which you are, but because you don't know how to recruit. As the employer, it's your job to hire the best people for the job. If they don't perform, it's also your responsibility to lead, manage and coach, which you won't know how to do or will use as a learning experience at the beginning of this journey.

Look for action, not what you're being told. If you can focus on your staff's efforts, you won't be blinded by the sparkling and shiny words they use to keep you happy. If you don't look for actions and only believe the words, chances are you've had a blindfold pulled over your eyes that's costing you more money than you'd like to accept.

I'm by no means saying all employees are feeding you lines. However, at the beginning of recruiting and hiring, pay attention to the work performed and the actions, not the words because you may not have learned this lesson yet.

It will save you heartache, money, and most importantly, time. Hire better and fire quicker.

I like to do 60- to 90-day trial periods for a new hire, with a clear agreement of what I expect and what the person expects of me before accepting the job. I learned this because I never did it, and learned that most entry-level employees put on a show for 90 days because they think that once 90-day marks are passed, they can in most cases collect unemployment after quitting or being fired. However, when you've gone through that lesson more than once, you learn to put contracts in place or use a written agreement that spells out what's expected of your new staff so there's no question.

I like to use a long employee manual and 90-day agreement or contract with our signatures to capture the deal. Don't get me wrong, not everyone will take advantage of you and most didn't of me, but after losing more money than I'd like to admit due to employees, you'd put these parameters in place too.

The real gold is knowing who you should hire, which starts with your job listing. You need a clear understanding of what you want to manifest as the ideal applicant. You should know who you want, and then who you want will see the ad and possibly be the match you're looking for.

Once you get new hires knowing what's expected of them, with proper onboarding, coaching and leadership, they might become loyal and dedicated to you and your vision. When that happens and you find good team members, do everything you can to hang on to them. If they're not that dedicated, coach them and sell them on your vision—that's your job as the owner.

Anyone who doesn't perform after corrective action and proper coaching needs to be fired…and fast, saving you money and time.

Hire better, fire much quicker and don't fall victim to their stories or feel bad for them because that's what they're banking on. This would be you feeling guilty for firing someone due to underperformance, not performing or worse, lying to you and the employee playing the victim card.

I learned that the hard way from someone who did all that, and did it very well. At the point of hiring, I'd gotten much better at recruiting after a few years of practice, but those who are used to manipulating and banking off of guilt know what they're doing, and they're great at it. They've done it their entire lives.

Early on, within his first two months, I received a sexual harassment complaint against him, and then he was arrested for theft. I spent a lot of time talking with him and hearing his story in both situations and, to his credit, his stories were believable and could have been true—I'll actually never know.

What I do know is "a zebra never loses his stripes" and "where there's smoke, there's fire." I saw two red flags and was watching closely. Remember, look for actions, never words.

As time went on, I received complaints from the staff about his girlfriend being hostile to the other team members when she'd call. I addressed the situation and was told it would never happen again. Guess what? You guessed it, more complaints of the same situation, including twice with me. Of course, when addressed, I'd be told it would never happen again. I pointed out that it did.

She was also using the gym while that employee was working and it made the rest of the staff uncomfortable. It wasn't fair that his girlfriend used the gym for free. No other family, friends or significant others did that, given my clear company policy, which was being violated. I was told it wouldn't happen again, and at that moment, I not only knew that it would happen again, but the next time it happened, I'd have to let him go, and I told him I would.

You might ask yourself how I knew it would happen again and the answer is in the patterns of the individual; numbers and patterns never lie, only people do. How often had he told me nothing would happen again versus how many times that happened created patterns through his actions. Pay close attention and save yourself money and time. He knew his job was on the line, so he got better at hiding it all.

I heard rumors she was still using the gym early in the morning before I got to work. When I addressed it, I was told it wasn't happening. But I'd already learned the lesson by hearing one of my morning openers may have been using drugs while at work. I arrived early one glorious morning to see for myself. What I found blew my mind, and I let him go.

Look for actions—look for patterns, not words that sound good. Hire better, fire quicker. Considering that I'd already learned this lesson about people being sneaky in the morning, I popped in early one day and wouldn't you know it? I see exactly who I was looking for and what I was told I wouldn't see in the gym—funny how that works.

Remember, where there's smoke, there's fire, and a zebra never loses his stripes. I let him go on the spot, and of course, he played the pity victim card.

Hire better, fire quicker. If employees aren't performing, coach them, teach them, lead them and if they continue to make the same mistakes, it isn't you as a mentor. It's their character and they must be let go to find their good elsewhere—quickly or they'll cost you a lot more than you'd like to give.

If you thought that story was bad, what I uncovered after the termination would make your skin crawl. Never take people or things for granted. Take them at face value, follow the actions, follow the data produced and remember that people lie. Numbers and actions don't.

PRO TIP: HIRE BETTER AND FIRE QUICKER

When I have employees who give it their best shot, are good humans and mean well but just can't get the job done, I try to have another job lined up for them where I think they'll fit better. When you go this far above and beyond to ensure someone's success, they'll respect you and always speak positively of you, and you'll create better in your life by selflessly giving when most humans won't. There have been several times I've done this for those who worked for me, and we're still in touch to celebrate their wins as their lives are evolving.

Terminating or losing a job doesn't have to be a negative experience. As the leader, the experience is what you as the coach and mentor make of it. If you end someone's job with negativity and harsh words, those words and actions will come back to haunt you. However, if you terminate with tactfulness, respect, honesty, empathy and loving words, you can create a relationship for life. Remember this when the time comes.

Actions, number and data speak louder than words, always.

As I rolled into my second year of gym ownership, knowing I was not on this earth to own and run gyms, we ironically picked up serious steam as a company. I was practicing on my staff, mentoring and coaching them, leading by example and living the life I preached as our vision because I knew my purpose was to teach.

I continued to learn, make mistakes and move on, as did my team. At this point, the team was solid; we had some heavy hitters who pulled their weight and stepped up to the plate, helping me when they saw how overextended I'd become growing the gym and also with my startup company, which was a whole other beast.

There was a local award that meant a lot to the team and members. It was called the "Best Gym of New Haven," which we badly wanted to win. But no one wanted it more than me.

I'd done a ton of research on creating a bulletproof culture in a large company—I thought 60 employees was a large group. I began implementing the ideas, leading by example because that has always been my leadership style. The customers—many we saw daily—and staff started to work harmoniously, respecting one another and the overall tone. The building's energy began to shift from cold to warm and then hot.

If you're interested in learning more about culture, I recommend *Delivering Happiness* by the late Tony Hsieh. At this point, we had it, and I was wondering if I should buckle down and buy a few more gyms because things had shifted. That great culture brought hope of the local award "The Best Gym of New Haven" that with the help of the community, customers and staff voting for us, we could take the coveted award away from the powerhouse up-and-coming national chain after 20 years of them winning the award.

We won.

After winning, I published a picture of myself and my two dogs, Penelope and Frank, sitting next to me as I was holding the award. I was an up-and-coming local celebrity with a lot of social attention, with thousands of likes and hundreds of shares on social media.

So, wouldn't you know it? A week or so later, about a half-dozen of the general managers from the local chain we took the award from showed up for a workout at my place. I walked up to them because I knew most of them and greeted them with a big smile and said, "What the hell are you doing here in my small gym?" They were getting their cars serviced down the street and heard we were the best, so they wanted to kill two birds with one stone. I'll always remember how proud I was and happy to have them there in good spirit.

Years later, as I write these words, I'm now friends with the chain's owners and have done large deals with them because they're great gym owners. I'm not going to kid you, that put a lot of wind in my sails, but going into year three of working 12 hours a day, seven days a week, 365 days a year with minimal time to myself, for vacations, family and friends was starting to catch up to me at 33 years old.

I'd also opened two more companies for a total of four and was focused on the fifth, which was still only written on paper and not yet implemented. I was burning out.

I collapsed a few times, went to the hospital a few times and knew something needed to change. I hung on, though, and stayed focused, giving it my all, but also backing off to balance my life a bit and take care of myself before any longer-term damage occurred to my health. That was the road I was traveling if I hadn't reassessed.

I was focused on my purpose; I wanted to teach up-and-coming entrepreneurs how to be monsters in life and business.

When I say "monsters," I mean machines that crush it at whatever it is they do. They dominate their industries. I knew I was going to be the best business coach and mentor one day—well, as soon as Tony Robbins retires. Once the summer of 2019 came, I smelled something in the air, something very off, something terrifying, something I knew was going to impact billions of people: I saw the recession coming. However, I thought it would hit in the fourth quarter of 2019, not the first quarter of 2020, as it was so gracefully masked by COVID as the "Great Reset."

I was considered a great gym operator. It was eye-opening when I was referred to that way by Thomas Plummer, the best gym consultant in the field since 1977, who said that publicly at his convention in front of hundreds of other gym owners.

Still, I was nose deep in many markets at that point in life. I love many things, including real estate, exotic cars, high-end timepieces, stocks and more.

I started to notice smoke and mirrors. I saw soccer moms who should be driving minivans driving Escalades and Range Rovers running premium octane gas. I noticed young couples living in half-million-dollar homes while collectively making less than $150,000. I saw inflation on high-end timepieces that shouldn't have been there, and the same with exotic cars.

Interest rates were low, banks were handing out loans, and often. It was pointed out that we were running fat, and I mean very fat—so fat, we couldn't sustain this economic growth much longer as I saw and smelled a reflection of the 2008 recession in the air. I rethought my business plan, with all signs pointed to a crushing blow to retail or brick-and-mortar businesses like a full-service gym with a lot of space and a low per-person price point.

I knew it couldn't be sustained with the dark times to come. I felt it in my energy, and I felt it in my soul.

RESTRUCTURING THE EMPIRE

I'd been planning the launch of Warrior Consulting the

following year. I was excited not because it was my fifth, but because I'd had this company on my goal board for the year and was finally doing it. For some reason, when I have long-term goals on my goal board, I get complacent, thinking I could accomplish them faster than the time that was needed. In reality, I was underestimating the time required…and reality set in. I was planning the company that aligned to my purpose as a teacher—the reason I'm on this earth.

As I wrote earlier, I knew owning gyms was only a stepping stone, as there were far more critical missions to accomplish. I knew this was it, and the impact would be far more significant than a 20,000-square-foot community gym serving a few thousand customers when I was on the brink of providing value for soon-to-be hundreds of thousands, then millions.

Only one of my four companies before the recession was brick and mortar. The others were virtual-based and highly adaptable to variables that could be thrown at them. To put this point in perspective, once the recession hit in 2020, the four virtual companies were up nearly 700% in revenue versus 2019.

That said, I felt in my energy the variables coming and was correctly planning for them. I began to build all-virtual companies diligently as 2019 ended, training new staff, building new processes, simplifying procedures and padding them for the economic hit to come. As you guessed, it drew back my energy on the brick-and-mortar aspect of my portfolio.

"Never sacrifice nine men to save one."
~ Thomas Plummer

The real gold was putting together lesson plans for group courses like this book, compiling the literature I'd planned to teach the next year. Once I publicly opened enrollment, I knew there would be many who wanted to learn from me, so I built three courses to run for 2020: Dominate Your Day, Leading Humans and Money Mindset and Sales.

But I was vastly wrong. I didn't beta test the market, assuming I'd only be hired by up-and-coming entrepreneurs, established entrepreneurs or those who thought they wanted to become an entrepreneur. What ended up happening was very different for the launch of Dominate Your Day.

To say I knew what I was doing would be a fallacy as I'd never taught publicly for pay, nor marketed or promoted a product either. As I marketed the system through March 2020, I noticed I'd made that mistake in assuming who would hire me—most who reached out for a spot in the first system were not entrepreneurs. Still, they were primarily men around my age looking for a mentor. That became the birth of my mentoring programs. I quickly adapted the material to focus on mentoring. It wasn't hard, just unexpected.

We as a company were soaring high with our presale and then simultaneously launching Warrior Consulting, what I felt back in the summer of 2019 was brought to fruition, disguised as a pandemic of COVID-19.

Before I continue, I want to clear up misinformation and assumptions of COVID-19. As I write these words nearly a year after the outbreak of COVID-19, no one can pinpoint whether this was born in a lab in China or not. There's a gray area of how this epidemic started and spread, but we do know the American people weren't ready for such an epidemic. And, the mainstream media, social media and everything in between did their best to scare the daylights out of everyone.

In contrast, people like me knew the underlying issue and the agenda to come. All in all, we have a global reset and the arguably most significant shift in global power and money since the fall of Rome. Our country left the door wide open for China, the new powerhouse on the block. As of 2020, one of the youngest countries on earth is no longer the world superpower. On the other hand, China, which has been around for millennia, is now the world superpower.

And just like that, on March 16th, at about 11:00 a.m., the Connecticut state governor announced on Facebook that we as a gym, along with an overpowering number of "nonessential" businesses, were to close our doors by 8:00 p.m. that night, with

CHRISTOPHER WARNES

no planned reopening date. We, the people of America, had to do our part in "flattening the curve," which we were told would last two weeks.

WHEN YOU KNOW IT'S TIME TO LET GO

With the amazing feats of online companies and the serious ground we were taking in that direction, we had our hands full with the gym.

Within a week, I had some of the toughest phone calls I've ever made. I knew I had to lay everyone off, other than a couple of key managers. I explained to my girlfriend how hard these phone calls were going to be. I'd put almost four years into building the team, which was a serious amount of energy, money and time. I was pacing back and forth, puking—drinking water that would come right back up.

The only people in my life who understood the circumstances were those who could relate by experience, having built a team and knowing firsthand how much energy goes into that. I felt like my words were mainly falling upon deaf ears.

Having my managers handle these phone calls didn't feel right, and I knew these were conversations I had to have, so I did. Over the next few months, knowing things would continue to get economically worse, I was still building and executing the virtual companies, while also attempting to shift the gym to a virtual company, which was a challenge.

I was watching the membership numbers we'd worked so diligently on over the past few years—growing our monthly electronic funds transfer from 1,770 members to nearing 3,000 at the time of COVID—just get demolished by freezes and cancelations. I decided to let the members out of their contracts. I didn't have to legally, but my ethics as a businessman have guided me since the military. Fairness is how I operate.

At times, some may not like the decisions, but fairness goes a long way in the long-term aspect of business and life. You can't please everyone, but do what's right for the masses not the select few who have a problem with your decision. Those

128

people more than likely have only problems in their lives and project those problems into yours.

Finally, four long months later, in late June of 2020, we were allowed to reopen to the public—of course with heavy stipulations and rules, understandably. However, what was only just being talked about publicly was how the economy was struggling due to the government-mandated shutdowns of commerce.

I should have permanently closed the doors to the gym because I knew there was no end in sight. I couldn't have been more right given the political structure of New England…let alone Connecticut.

But I decided to reopen and hang on, giving it our best shot. I called my staff back up and, to my delight, 99% wanted their jobs back, with just a few who didn't feel comfortable given their personal health situations. In hindsight, I gave it the best shot, not for me, but for our members and my beloved staff. I was dead-set on keeping the doors open so they could put food on their tables.

Then, more smoke and mirrors came.

The first week we were open, we sold about 100 new memberships, which was similar to a decent month of "normal" membership sales for comparison.

On the other hand, the cancelations of memberships continued at an alarming rate. Many people were scared of the COVID propaganda blasted through the media outlets, but what really killed us was what I felt in my energy nearly a year earlier: The recession was hitting hard as the gym market was made up primarily of entry-level workers making enough to get by until they were fired or laid off.

Now, what happens when people lose a job? Most of the time, savings are minimal and they go into scarcity mode, scared, not knowing what they're going to do for money. They cut back on unnecessary expenses, like gym memberships.

Within a month, I thought I was going to have to cut it off. Nothing was going to get better. At the 60-day mark, I'd been bleeding money for almost six months and finally, at the 90-day mark in late August, I mustered up the courage to call my attorneys and tell them it was over. That tough phone call set the precedence for more challenging phone calls, social posts and much more to come over the next 30 days.

By late August, I'd finally accepted the inevitable, the decision I should have made on March 16th, 2020, when the state of Connecticut, under an executive order, mandated that our industry close.

The most challenging part of the entire life-changing situation of letting go wasn't the financial impact. It wasn't letting my staff go; it wasn't closing the gym to members and wasn't the fear of judgment, although that was a close second. It wasn't anything other than me trying to reframe my thoughts. My ego was doing an excellent job at distorting the truth to myself. I had to fight myself to accept, finally, after countless journal sessions, meditation speaking to my higher self, verbal prayer and an abundance of affirmations, I had done nothing wrong.

This is a prime example of the 99-to-1 rule on display. This lesson was undoubtedly the hardest I learned during my business career and will always be an example of how I held on too long, thinking I could fix a problem when the issue of a global pandemic and government-mandated shutdown was far beyond my control. High performers tend to deal with challenging situations head-on and, from time to time, struggle with acceptance of temporary defeat.

If you're struggling to relate to a situation of the right time to let go, try to look at it this way. Let's say you've never had a business, let alone had to shut one down after you put energy into eight years of seven days a week, 365 days a year up to 22 hours a day, all your life savings, sleepless nights, pain, blood, lost relationships, anxiety, early mornings, late nights, destroyed taxes and years without pay, but you have a family that means the world to you.

One day the local government comes along and rips them away from you, then starves them in front of you, so they're no longer on this earth, but you have to stay alive to watch.

I hope no one has to go through a situation like this and only wish the impact of the words resonate for those who have never closed a business but now can relate to what a business needs, which is customers. Without customers, a business can't eat and if the company can't eat because the local government makes a declaration, it dies no matter how hard you work to save your life's work.

The exciting thing about the global pandemic and how greatly it affected commerce during these times for America is this: Governments, local and federal, and businesses have to keep a harmonious relationship with one another to survive. The government relies completely on large businesses to fund itself. Yes, our government depends upon business to survive. The simple word is "tax."

On the other hand, business depends on government to control the environment, not allowing monopolies complete control over an industry, which has happened in America. It raised my eyebrow when we were given the order to close, which might not even be legal. That said, I see both sides and only know the choice I had was to follow our governor's orders because I thought that was the best decision.

BRINGING THE LESSON FULL CIRCLE

No matter a situation, business or personal, we must understand when something is no longer serving us, aligned to us, on our frequency or isn't a vibrational match for us.

The key to the lesson is having the ability to understand ourselves well enough to know what best serves us and what we're vibrationally aligned to.

Most humans avoid the tough inner look into themselves to understand their being, their soul and who they are. It can be frightening. We have to understand what makes us tick, why we are and who we are.

What we see in the mirror isn't who we are. It's only the vessel we occupy in this life—much like driving a car to and from work, your body is your transport for this life.

Who you are is not your name. It's not the hand you see. It's far beyond that, which the conscious mind can show only when we decide to face ourselves…the trauma, the shadow, the darkness, the wrongdoing of ourselves and others.

Only when we continue to face ourselves will we understand what's best aligned to us in this life. And when we understand what's best aligned to us, we'll know when it's time to let go of whatever we want out of our lives. To hold the door open for what's exciting, smile, wave and give up and trust that the universe is always watching and will put and take all that's right for you when you're ready to give and receive.

Before we move on to the conclusion, I'll tell the story about the final 30 days before officially closing the doors to my gym. I'd given up and trusted that all would be. I was no longer fighting as I did for the nine months prior, thinking I could fix the problem when in reality I should have just let go. It was a tough time. If I could relate the pain and anguish, it was comparable to the day I spoke of in the opening chapter of this book, June 18th, 2006, when I was wounded in combat.

However, there was a massive difference in these pains. Physical pain is the easiest to understand and fix as, in a micro sense, you need to change, then heal. Emotional, spiritual, financial, doubt and anxiety was a much different beast to deal with as it was multifaceted and was the driving force of my thoughts. Outside of the type of pain, the major difference was that of defeat versus failure.

In 2006, I'd given up; I decided there was nothing more I could do and so I and three others were evacuated off the battlefield. This was long before my spiritual journey. I was a mere boy of 21.

At 35, my mindset was far more advanced, as was the rest of my life. As the day neared when I publicly addressed my staff, customers and friends, something very freeing yet also odd happened. I'd given up and trusted that the universe was supplying me with my unlimited supply of all. Within a week, I closed my gym, ended a long-term relationship and parted ways with a mentor. Any one of these situations has wreaked havoc on people, let alone ruined their lives and to an extreme degree has pushed people over the edge to end their lives.

I remained calm, I remained grateful for my life; I remained hopeful, and I KNEW the universe was the source of my unlimited supply, taking anything from me no longer aligned and putting into my life what is aligned. I'm a fortunate man for the relationships built and forged. The people who have always been closest to me, in my corner for decades, came out of the woodwork to come check on me.

The irony struck me as a bit odd. However, I understood; many said they'd be there and do anything needed over the years they were in my life. They were the first to turn their backs and leave when they thought there was nothing more to take and I understand they made that decision. Humans can be good at manipulating how you see them and will work, not even consciously at times, but are programmed subconsciously to keep you convinced of who they are.

Remember these two examples: They haven't taken the journey to understand themselves to the depths needed—and they might not ever—and often don't even know what they're doing or who they're abusing with their behavior. Their selfish behavior is the route to their less-than-ideal patterns.

And secondly, actions speak louder than words. Look at actions and data. The numbers never lie. People do. Where there's smoke, there's fire, and a zebra never loses his stripes.

The fitness field was a great stepping stone for me in the direction of much larger proportions. I'm thankful for the four years I had as a top-performing gym owner, the people I met, and most importantly, the lessons learned along the way. I wouldn't be writing these words today if it wasn't for the constant fight to succeed as a gym owner.

I'll always remain grateful for every mistake made, every misfortune that happened, every relationship that no longer serves me, every day worked to achieve the dream I had in the screen of my mind.

That turned into reality for four great years of learning exactly what I didn't want in life, creating the vehicle that drove me to take the cumbersome step toward my new life and the burning desire to change humanity, leaving this world just a bit better than when I arrived in 1985.

The unaligned path created the mountain to climb of purpose and a life full of embracing purpose to give back and teach others through my mistakes. I want to teach them that they can achieve their wildest dreams.

You, too, can live a life so incredibly rewarding when you have a burning desire to accomplish all you can. I'm a grateful man, and my hope is that you can harness a gratitude, burning desire and purpose to change your life.

If this speaks to you, if it lands with you, if it resonates with you, get up, dream up a plan, write it down and execute that plan as such that you'd rather die than not take a step forward toward creating all you dream of.

I'm cheering for you. Let's win together.

ACKNOWLEDGMENTS

I'd like to take a moment and express the gratitude that runs through me for the many people who supported, encouraged and helped me during the creation of this book that started as a vivid meditation and ended with the start of a legacy.

Thank you to my best friend, Steven Taft, and his amazing wife, Tracy, who not only suppor1ted me in writing this book, but also donated their time and expertise, editing this book more than once. I wouldn't have asked anyone else to be the first to read, let alone edit, keeping my tone intact to help others realize they can develop the life they dream of. It was an honor to stand next to you in your wedding as your best man and I hope I continue to serve you both and make you proud with what we've accomplished together.

To my assistant Paola, who handled everything I couldn't do, day in and day out, never taking a sick day or complaining of the mountain-load of work to accomplish so I could create this book, I am and always will be in debt to you. Please know how much I appreciate you, all you have done, and the sacrifices you've made in an effort to bring to life my vision, of which you have seen. Thank you.

Thanks to my team for constantly making sure I had what was needed to focus on this project and be able to meet deadlines while writing. Without you, this book wouldn't have been written. Thank you from the bottom of my heart.

A huge thank you to my students at Warrior Consulting, listening to drafts of the book in our classes, loving the content and encouraging me to finish so they can read it. You rock— thank you for being you. Onward and upward!

Lastly, thank you to my mother, Nanci, who has supported me in everything I set my mind to from day one. Mom, you've provided me with an incredible amount of love and support, not only during this process but also through life. I owe it all to you and am forever grateful for the life you've provided me.

Much love to you all.

Made in the USA
Las Vegas, NV
06 December 2023

82209954R00075